The Schoolwide Enrichment Model in Science

The Schoolwide Enrichment Model in Science

A Hands-On Approach for Engaging Young Scientists

Nancy N. Heilbronner, Ph.D.,
& Joseph S. Renzulli, Ed.D.

PRUFROCK PRESS INC.
WACO, TEXAS

Library of Congress Cataloging-in-Publication Data

Names: Renzulli, Joseph S., author. | Helibronner, Nancy N., 1957- author.
Title: The schoolwide enrichment model in science : a hands-on approach for engaging young scientists / by Joseph S. Renzulli and Nancy N. Helibronner.
Description: Waco, Texas : Prufrock Press Inc., 2016.
Identifiers: LCCN 2015029567 (print) | LCCN 2015042116 (ebook) | ISBN 9781618214997 (pbk.) | ISBN 9781618215000 (pdf) | ISBN 9781618215017 (ePub)
Subjects: LCSH: Science--Study and teaching--United States. | Gifted children--Education--United States. | Curriculum planning--United States.
Classification: LCC Q181 .R475 2016 (print) | LCC Q181 (ebook) | DDC 507.1/2073--dc23
LC record available at http://lccn.loc.gov/2015029567

Edited by Lacy Compton

Cover design by Raquel Trevino and layout design by Allegra Denbo

ISBN-13: 978-1-61821-499-7

Printed in the United States of America.

Prufrock Press Inc.
P.O. Box 8813
Waco, TX 76714-8813
Phone: (800) 998-2208
Fax: (800) 240-0333
http://www.prufrock.com

Table of Contents

CHAPTER 1

Understanding the Gifted Learner

Theoretical and Research Background Underlying the Schoolwide Enrichment Model in Science

How can we develop high levels of interest, engagement, and enthusiasm for scientific inquiry in young people? What services should be provided to all students and what opportunities, resources, and encouragement should be provided to students with special interests and aptitudes for advanced-level scientific work? The Schoolwide Enrichment Model in Science (SEM-Science) was developed to address these two questions. In this chapter, a chronology of how the SEM model was developed, a description of the original Enrichment Triad Model, and a summary of pertinent research highlights are presented (Renzulli & Reis, 1994).

The SEM promotes engagement through the use of three types of enrichment experiences that are enjoyable, challenging, and interest-based, and the SEM-Science extends and applies that model into science. Separate studies on the SEM have demonstrated its effectiveness in schools with widely differing socioeconomic levels and program organization patterns (Olenchak, 1988; Olenchak & Renzulli, 1989). The SEM was developed using Renzulli's Enrichment Triad Model (Renzulli, 1977; Renzulli & Reis, 1985, 1997, 2014) as a core. It has been implemented in thousands of schools across the country (Burns, 1998) and interest in this approach has continued to expand internationally. The effectiveness of the SEM has been studied in more than 30 years of research and field-tests, suggesting that the model is effective at serving high-ability students and providing enrichment in a variety of educational settings, including schools serving culturally diverse and low-socioeconomic populations.

A Brief History of the SEM

The original Enrichment Triad Model (Renzulli, 1976), the curriculum core underlying the SEM, was developed in the mid-1970s and initially implemented as a gifted and talented programming model. The model, initially field-tested in several districts, proved to be quite popular and requests from all over the country for visitations to schools using the model and for information about how to implement the model increased. A book about the Enrichment Triad Model (Renzulli, 1977) was published, and increasing numbers of districts began implementing this approach. It was at this point that a clear need was established for research about the effectiveness of the model and for other vehicles that could provide technical assistance for interested educators to help develop programs in their schools. Different types of programs based on the Enrichment Triad were designed and implemented by classroom, gifted education, and enrichment teachers. In some of these programs, the focus was on many different types of introductory enrichment, such as speakers, presentations, films, and other enrichment exposure opportunities. In others, the focus was on process skills, such as problem solving and critical and creative problem solving. In some Triad programs, high levels of student creative productivity occurred, while in others, few students engaged in this type of work. In some programs, enrichment opportunities were offered to students not formally identified for the enrichment program, while in others, only identified "gifted" students had any access to enrichment experiences. Some teachers and coordinators were extremely successful in implementing the model, while others were not. Certain professional development opportunities and resources proved to be extremely helpful in enabling some teachers to better implement the program, and staff development opportunities were provided to make enrichment services available to larger numbers of teachers and students. And, of course, increasing interest in why the model was working and how we could further expand the research base of this approach led to almost 30 years of field-testing, research, and dissemination.

Present efforts to develop giftedness are based on a long history of previous theoretical or research studies dealing with human abilities (Sternberg, 1984, 1988, 1990; Sternberg & Davidson, 1986; Thorndike, 1921) and a few general conclusions from the most current research on giftedness (Sternberg & Davidson, 2005) provide a critical background for this discussion of the SEM-Science. The first is that giftedness is not a unitary concept, but there are many manifestations of gifts and talents and therefore single definitions cannot adequately explain this multifaceted phenomenon. The confusion about present theories of giftedness has led many researchers to develop new models for explaining this complicated concept, but most agree that giftedness is developed over time and that culture, abilities, environment, gender, opportunities, and chance contribute to the development of gifts and talents (Sternberg & Davidson, 2005).

The SEM-Science focuses on both traditional scientific academic development and the development of creative productive giftedness in the area of science. Creative productive giftedness describes those aspects of human activity and involvement where a premium is placed on the development of original material and products that are purposefully designed to have an impact on one or more target audiences. Learning situations designed to promote creative productive giftedness emphasize the use and application of information (content) and thinking skills in an integrated, inductive, and real-problem-oriented manner. In the SEM, traditional academic gifts are developed using curriculum compacting, acceleration, differentiated instruction, and various forms of academic enrichment. Our focus on creative productivity complements our efforts to increase academic challenge when we attempt to transform the role of the student from that of a learner of lessons to one of a firsthand inquirer who can experience the joys and frustrations of creative productivity (Renzulli, 1977). This approach is quite different from the development of giftedness that tends to emphasize deductive learning, advanced content and problem solving, and the acquisition, storage, and retrieval of information. In other words, creative productive giftedness enables children to work on issues and areas of study that have personal relevance to the student and can be escalated to appropriately challenging levels of investigative activity.

Why is creative productive giftedness important enough to question the traditional approach that has been used to select students for gifted programs on the basis of test scores? Why do some people want to rock the boat by challenging a conception of giftedness that can be numerically defined by simply giving a test? The answers to these questions are simple and yet compelling. A review of research literature (Neisser, 1979; Reis & Renzulli, 1982; Renzulli, 1978, 1986, 2005) tells us that there is much more to identifying human potential than the abilities revealed on traditional tests of intelligence, aptitude, and achievement. Furthermore, history tells us it has been the creative and productive people of the world, the producers rather than consumers of knowledge who have been recognized in history as "truly gifted" individuals. Accordingly, the SEM integrates opportunities for both academic giftedness and creative productive giftedness.

Three-Ring Conception of Giftedness

The SEM-Science is based on Renzulli's (1978) Three-Ring Conception of Giftedness, which defines gifted behaviors rather than gifted individuals. This conception encompasses three interrelated components (see Figure 1) and is described as follows:

> Gifted behavior consists of behaviors that reflect an interaction among three basic clusters of human traits—above average ability, high levels of task commitment, and high levels of creativity. Individuals capable of developing gifted behavior are those possessing or capable of developing this composite set of traits and applying them to any potentially valuable area of human performance. Persons who manifest or are capable of developing an interaction among the three clusters require a wide variety of educational opportunities and services that are not ordinarily provided through regular instructional programs. (Renzulli, 2002, p. 69)

Longitudinal research supports this distinction between academic giftedness and creative productive giftedness. Perleth, Sierwald, and Heller (1993) found differences between students who demonstrated creative productive as opposed to traditional academic giftedness. Most of the confusion and controversy surrounding the definitions of giftedness can be placed into perspective if we examine a few key questions. Is giftedness or creativity an absolute or a relative concept (Amabile, 1983)? That is, is a person either gifted or not gifted (the absolute view), or can varying degrees of gifted behaviors be developed in certain people, at certain times, and under certain circumstances (the relative view)? Is giftedness or creativity a static concept (i.e., you have or you don't have it) or is it a dynamic concept (i.e., it varies within persons, cultures, and among learning/performance situations)?

These questions have led us to advocate a fundamental change in the ways we believe that the concept of giftedness should be viewed. For 30 years, we have advocated *labeling the services students receive rather than labeling the students*, for we believe that a shift should occur from an emphasis on the traditional concept of "being gifted" (or not being gifted) to a concern about the *development of gifted and creative behaviors* in students who have high potential for benefiting from special educational opportunities, as well as the provision of some types of enrichment for all students. This change in terminology may also provide the

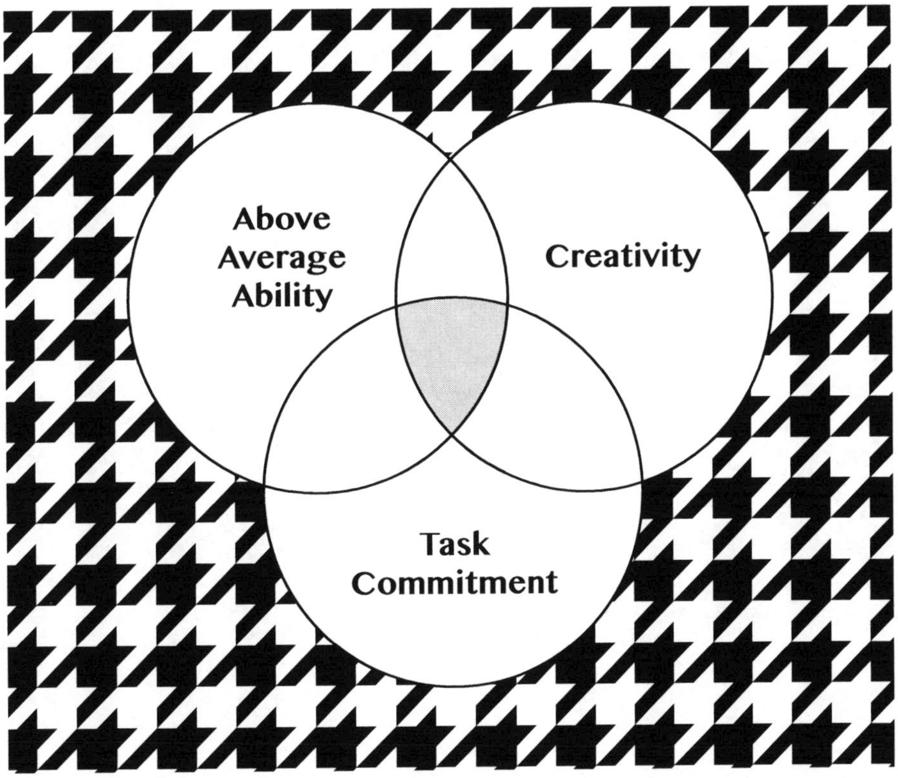

Figure 1. Three-ring conception of giftedness. *Note.* The houndstooth background reflects the interactive influences of personality and environment.

flexibility in both identification and programming endeavors that encourages the inclusion of at-risk and underachieving students in our programs. Our ultimate goal is the development of a total school enrichment program that benefits all students and concentrates on *making schools places for talent development for all young people.*

The Enrichment Triad Model

The Triad Model (Renzulli, 1977), the curricular basis of the SEM, was originally designed as a gifted program model to encourage creative productivity on the parts of young people by exposing them to various topics, areas of interest, and fields of study, and to further train them to *apply* advanced content, process-training skills, and methodology training to self-selected areas of interest using three types of enrichment. The original Triad Model with three types of

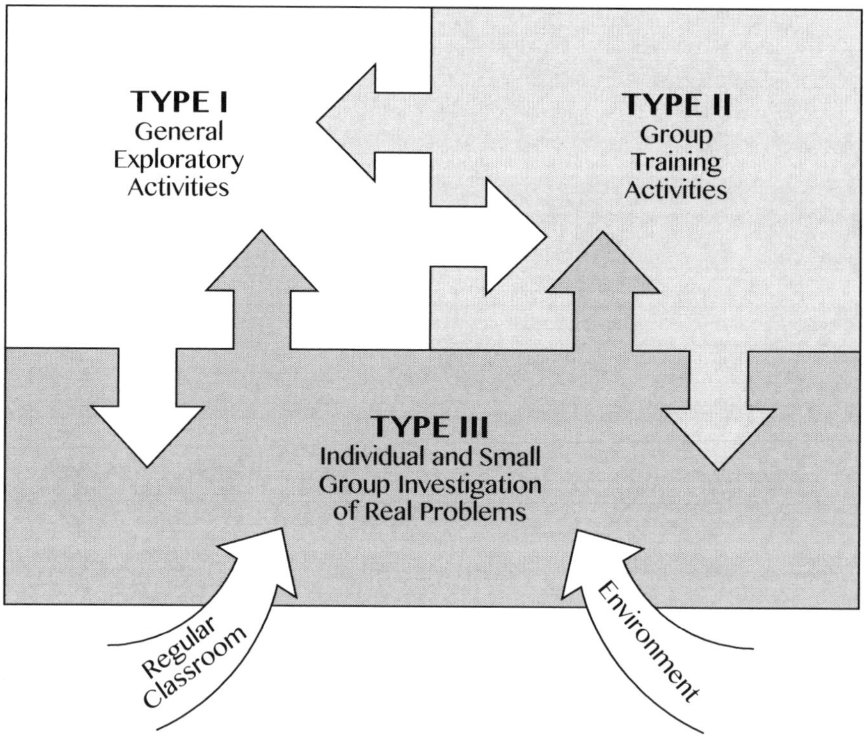

Figure 2. The Enrichment Triad Model.

enrichment (see Figure 2) was implemented in programs designed for academically talented and gifted students.

In the Enrichment Triad Model, Type I Enrichment is designed to expose students to a wide variety of disciplines, topics, occupations, hobbies, persons, places, and events that would not ordinarily be covered in the regular curriculum. In schools using this approach, an enrichment team of parents, teachers, and students often organizes and plans Type I experiences by contacting speakers, arranging minicourses, conducting overviews of enrichment clusters, demonstrations, performances, using Internet resources, or by ordering and distributing films, slides, CDs and DVDs, or other print or nonprint media. Type I Enrichment is mainly designed to stimulate new interests leading to Type II or III follow-up on the parts of students who become motivated by Type I experiences. Type I Enrichment can be provided by Type I experiences. Type I Enrichment can be provided for general groups, or for students who have already expressed an interest in the topic area.

Type II Enrichment includes materials and methods designed to promote the development of thinking and feeling processes. Some Type II Enrichment is general, and usually provided to groups of students in their classrooms or in enrichment programs. This general Type II training includes the development of (a) creative thinking and problem solving, critical thinking, and affective processes; (b) a wide variety of specific learning how-to-learn skills; (c) skills in the appropriate use of advanced-level reference materials; and (d) written, oral, and visual communication skills. Other Type II Enrichment is specific, as it cannot be planned in advance and usually involves advanced instruction in an interest area selected by the student. For example, students who become interested in botany after a Type I on this topic would pursue advanced training in this area by reading advanced content in botany; compiling, planning, and carrying out plant experiments; and more advanced methods training for those who want to go further and pursue a Type III in that area (Renzulli, 1982).

Type III Enrichment involves students who become interested in pursuing a self-selected area and are willing to commit the time necessary for advanced content acquisition and process training in which they assume the role of a firsthand inquirer. The goals of Type III Enrichment are:

- providing opportunities for applying interests, knowledge, creative ideas, and task commitment to a self-selected problem or area of study;
- acquiring advanced-level understanding of the knowledge (content) and methodology (process) that are used within particular disciplines, artistic areas of expression, and interdisciplinary studies;
- developing authentic products that are primarily directed toward bringing about a desired impact upon a specified audience;
- developing self-directed learning skills in the areas of planning, organization, resource utilization, time management, decision making, and self-evaluation; and
- the development of task commitment, self-confidence, and feelings of creative accomplishment.

An example using Next Generation Science Standards (NGSS Lead States, 2013). Type III products can be completed by individual or small groups of students and are always based on students' interests. Let's take an example we know, one based on the stories of thousands of students who have completed Type III investigations. Along the way, we'll be referencing a current body of standards that many school districts are using, the Next Generation Science Standards (NGSS; NGSS Lead States, 2013). Developed by the National

Research Council and meant to be a guide for science education, the standards are organized by content and also by practices. Standards of each type are referenced in the example provided below. All standards mentioned throughout the book are connected to an activity that is described, and all standards are cross-referenced to their activities in Appendix A.

Maria was always interested in the world around her, and nothing interested her more than taking things apart and putting them back together again. When she was younger, she took apart her family's household appliances, and when she grew older, it was her family's old computer that was the focus of her efforts. She even took apart things she shouldn't have—once she dismantled the engine of an old family car! When asked why she did these things, she always responded, "I just wanted to see how they worked inside." Recognizing an innate interest in engineering, Maria's teacher, Mr. D., brought in several engineers to speak with the class about projects they had undertaken (Type I experience). Excited, Maria asked one of the engineers, Dr. S., if she could work with her on developing a Type III project in engineering. When asked what she had in mind, Maria replied that for some time now she had been wondering if she could design a soundproof dog crate for the family's pet, Lucky. It seemed that Lucky barked whenever the family left the home, even if only for an hour, and Maria thought a soundproof crate would solve the problem (NGSS Crosscutting Practice 1—Defining Problems). Intrigued, Dr. S. agreed to work with Maria.

The two met weekly after school, and each time, Maria would propose different solutions. The crate would need to be safe and comfortable for Lucky, but it would need to be soundproof (NGSS Standard MS-PS4-2—Develop a model to describe that waves are reflected, absorbed, or transmitted through various materials.). Maria proposed insulating the crate with a heavy material, but Dr. S. pointed out that would make the crate hot. It would be best, Dr. S. suggested, if the dog could be seen in the crate, in case she was in distress. Dr. S. pointed Maria toward some information on soundproofing, including noise-cancelling technology. Maria eagerly read whatever information Dr. S. sent her way, and then she started going out on her own. She learned to use advanced resources such as electronic databases to locate articles on the topic (Type II skill). Each week, she would discuss what she had found with Dr. S. At last, she hit upon an idea for a material that was transparent and would muffle, if not completely eliminate, the barking. She then turned her attention to how to attach the material and how to ensure that air could flow into and out of the crate. Dr. S. suggested that she make a model using some lighter weight material and test it out (NGSS Crosscutting Practice 2—Developing Models), and so Maria made a miniature "dog crate," took temperatures inside the model and used a sound meter to measure the soundproofing quality of the materials (NGSS Crosscutting Practice 3—Planning Investigations and NGSS Crosscutting 4—Analyzing and Interpreting Data). Once the model tested satisfactorily, Dr. S. taught her how to use mathematics to consider temperature and soundproofing in the full-sized version (NGSS Crosscutting Practice 5—Using Mathematics and Computational Thinking). After completing the predictions, she built the full-size version, even including some new chew toys attached to the inside of the crate to keep Lucky busy and happy (NGSS Crosscutting Practice 6—Designing Solutions). She decided to test the crate with Lucky over short periods of time. Lucky used the crate only one minute the first time, with Maria carefully observing and taking notes. During this period, whenever Lucky barked, Maria tested the sound level of the noise using a decibel meter. Lucky seemed to like the crate—he could see out, and he especially enjoyed the new toys. Maria like it, because when she walked out, the sounds coming from the crate were muffled. Her idea worked! Maria tested it over longer periods, and because Lucky showed no signs of distress and the sound was muffled, her Type III product was deemed a success (NGSS Crosscutting Practice 7—Engaging in Argument From Evidence). Maria and Dr. S considered next steps: how to improve and possibly market the soundproof crate for dog owners who lived in apartments everywhere (NGSS Crosscutting Practice 8—Obtaining, Evaluating and Communicating Evidence).

Type III Enrichment is designed to guide students through investigative and creative processes that make use of exposure to new and interesting topics resulting from Type I Enrichment and the thinking skills developed from the Type II training activities described above. Type III Enrichment consists of individual and small-group projects that are guided by the following four principles:

1. Personalization of interest
2. Use of authentic investigative and creative methodology
3. No single predetermined correct answer or prescribed way of pursuing the problem
4. Designed to have an impact on selected audiences

Type III Enrichment casts the learner in the role of a practicing professional, even if at a more junior level than adult researchers, writers, and artists. This highest type of enrichment is designed to teach learners how to apply knowledge by becoming a firsthand investigator, creative artist or designer, or leader in an action-oriented project.

The Theory of Blended Knowledge

The Triad Model is based on a theory of knowledge that that emphasizes the blending of Received Knowledge, Analyzed Knowledge, and Applied and Created Knowledge (see Figure 3) and that dates back to the times of the ancient Greeks (Reis, 2015). Before describing this theory, it is important first to discuss two related issues that are part of the rationale underlying the theory. The theory deals with both sources of information and the three main categories of knowledge typically discussed in the literature on epistemology. Who and what are the providers of information and knowledge in formal learning situations? When it comes to schooling, there are essentially two major sources of knowledge. The first source is defined as To-Be-Presented (T-B-P) knowledge, and this type is usually transmitted to students through lectures, textbooks, and other forms of print, visual, or auditory media. Committees that develop curricular standards and textbook writers almost universally determine what T-B-P knowledge is used in today's schools, and it is also highly influenced by persons who develop standardized tests. Most traditional learning is based on this source of knowledge.

The second source of knowledge is Just-In-Time (J-I-T) Knowledge, and this is the type of knowledge that people only "go and get" because it is necessary to address a particular problem or to learn more about something that is assigned or of personal interest to the individual. The advent of technology and the Internet has now made access to J-I-T Knowledge readily available to most teachers and students. Technology has also provided us with software that can personalize learning in a way never before available, and it can personalize learning beyond merely modifying the amount and level of content provided to students. A program developed at the University of Connecticut (Field, 2009; Renzulli & Reis, 2007) creates an individual profile for each student based on his or her interests, learning styles, and preferred modes of expressions, and a unique search engine analyzes each profile to match high engagement resources according to the ways students have responded to the questionnaire that generates the profile. Teachers can also use this software to review, select, and infuse high engagement enrichment activities into selected curricular topics or units of study being pursued by individuals, small groups, or entire classrooms. True personalization of learning is now possible through the use of today's technology, and teachers now have at their disposal the tools that allow them to blend together the three types of knowledge described below.

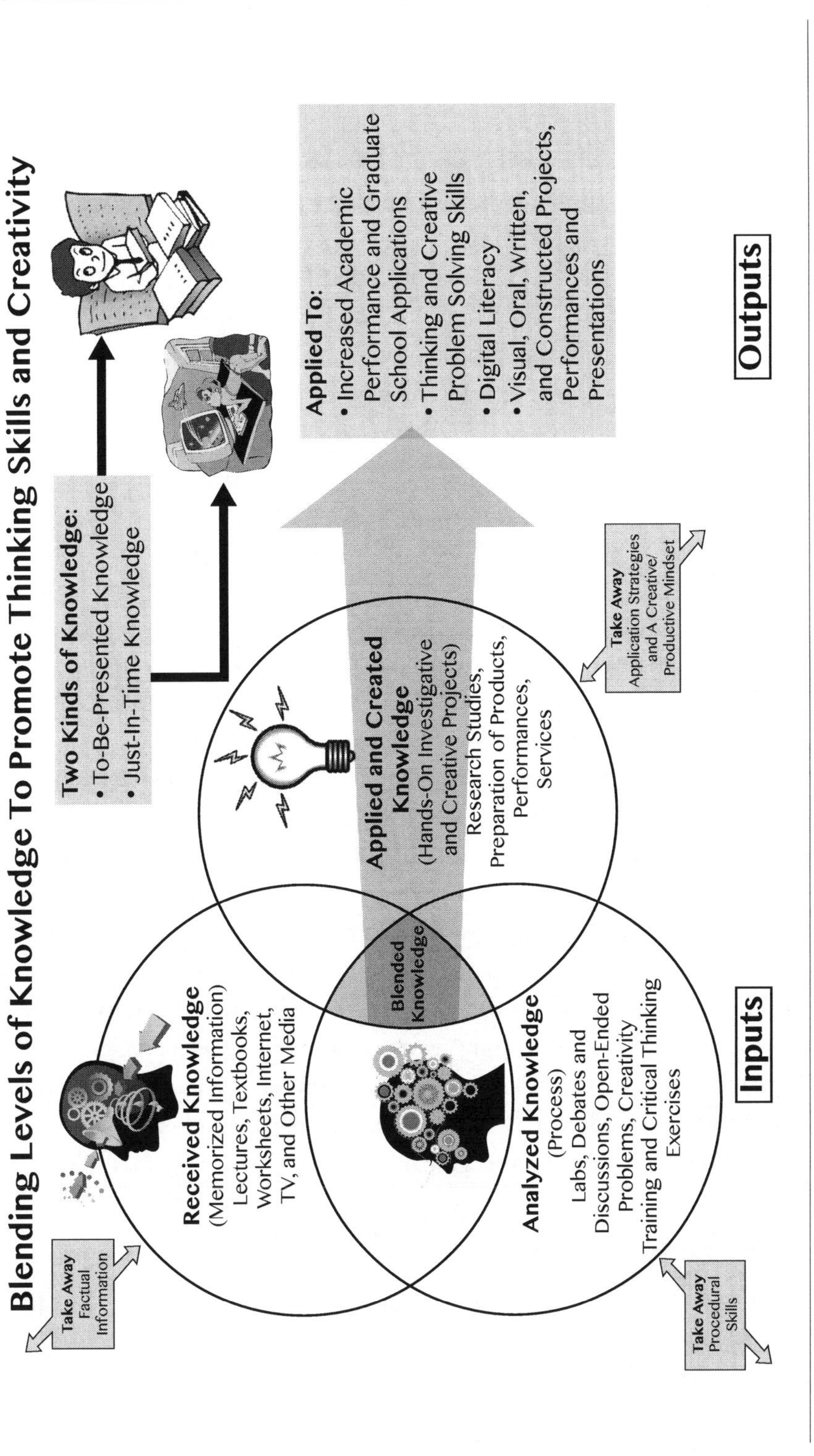

Figure 3. Theory of Blended Knowledge: Received, Analyzed, and Applied and Created Knowledge.

Adults in most practical, work related, and problem-solving situations use J-I-T Knowledge routinely and now the advent of easy-to-use digital age technology has now made J-I-T Knowledge readily accessible to most school-age learners. For example, a middle school student investigating the reasons for the collapse of a large building used National Weather Bureau data to obtain the snow accumulations and temperature records for his region of the country over a 50-year period. He also obtained building code regulations and hypothesized that weight-bearing regulations written decades earlier were insufficient to accommodate present-day large roof building designs. Imagine how dreadfully boring and irrelevant it would be if all students were required to learn or even memorize 50 years of weather data? The student conducting this study needed the information and therefore it became instantaneously relevant.

Today's students are growing up in a world where their access to and familiarity with mobile devices provides them with instant entrée to the wider world of knowledge. The warp-speed technological changes taking place in schools today have become one of the few pervasive occurrences having a significant impact on the education system, so much so that technology is actually influencing learning theory itself. Consequently, technology has provided the necessary impetus to reassess the traditional methods and techniques that we use to bring knowledge into the classroom and guide students in its use.

Although philosophers and epistemologists have written for centuries about the general nature of knowledge, the theory presented here is restricted to the acquisition, application, and creation of knowledge in formal (schoolhouse) learning. Thus, the main "ingredients" for developing young minds mentioned above (information, knowledge, and the creative application of knowledge) can be categorized into the three general levels of knowledge depicted in Figure 3. Before describing each of these three levels, it should be emphasized that while they are hierarchical in level of complexity so far as the powers of mind are concerned (c.f., Bloom's hierarchy), it is the *interaction* between and among all three levels that creates the blended knowledge that is represented in the center of the three concentric circles in Figure 3.

Received Knowledge

The first level of knowledge is Received Knowledge, and this is the type of material most often associated with what traditional schooling is all about. At this level, information and knowledge are frequently used synonymously; however, leading knowledge scholars define small differences (Machlup, 1980). Information captures data at a single point and refers to material that has been given some meaning by way of a relational connection (e.g., Boston and Atlanta are state capital cities). Knowledge is the concise and appropriate collection of information in a way that makes it useful. Knowledge refers to a deterministic process where patterns within a given set of information are ascertained (capital cities are seats of government).

Received Knowledge such as facts, data, vocabulary, numeracy, names, dates, and other types of information are typically conveyed to students through lectures, textbooks, worksheets, and various types of digital media. It is the type of information that is usually assessed through standardized achievement tests or "right answer" tests constructed by teachers. Received Knowledge is the foundation for all learning and thus an essential component of the blended knowledge concept that makes up the center of Figure 3. Although memorization, note-taking skills, and recall are the main mental process developed for the acquisition of Received Knowledge, teachers have used attractive materials, the media, and a variety of classroom organization and management techniques to convert "raw" information into meaningful knowledge, and creative teachers have devised ways to make this level of knowledge more interesting and useful to students.

Analyzed Knowledge

The second level of knowledge and the type that has frequently been associated with programs for the gifted is Analyzed Knowledge. This level of knowledge has grown in popularity in recent years due to the focus on 21st-century thinking skills, the process standards included in the Common Core State Standards (National Governors Association Center for Best Practices & Council of Chief State School Officers, 2010), and the Next Generation Science Standards (NGSS; 2013), developed by the National Research Council, the National Science Teachers Association, and the American Association for the Advancement of Science. Kaplan (2009) discussed how this level of knowledge contributes to the depth and complexity that should be a hallmark of curriculum for gifted students. Analyzed Knowledge develops thinking skills such as: interpreting; extrapolating; recognizing attributes; discriminating between same and different; comparing and contrasting; categorizing; classifying; determining criteria; ranking, prioritizing, and sequencing; seeing relationships; determining cause and effect; pattern finding; and making analogies. These skills are typically associated with Bloom's higher level thinking categories of analysis, synthesis, and evaluation (Bloom, 1954).

Classroom practices that promote Analyzed Knowledge are much more advanced than merely receiving, storing, and retrieving information. Discussions, debates, simulations, role-playing, critiquing, and questioning that focus on attitudes, values, conclusions, and why, how, and cause-and-effect are typically the ways in which analysis skills are developed. Analyzed Knowledge obviously draws upon Received Knowledge, but it also interacts with Received Knowledge in a cyclical manner. When students are working at the analysis level, they may find the need to acquire ("go back") and obtain additional factual information to further examine or scrutinize an argument, point of view, or interpretation of a problem they are addressing. If Received Knowledge is "grist for the mill of mind," then Analyzed Knowledge is the "relentless grinding" of information that uses Received Knowledge to develop more complex levels of understanding.

Applied and Created Knowledge

These first two levels of knowledge are both priorities for all of our students. The ability to solve problems evolves from retrieving facts, data, and information and manipulating this material in ways that create meaning for the individual and improve the powers of mind. More advanced levels of problem solving and the construction of knowledge, however, require curiosity, creativity, and task commitment (Renzulli, 1982) to pursue problems that go beyond acquisition, prescribed problems, and even teacher-assigned problem-based learning activities. These traits should be the focus of programs for developing giftedness, and they should constitute the mission of gifted education mentioned above—increasing the world's reservoir of highly creative and productive individuals. It is this broader set of skills that develops the investigative, creative, and entrepreneurial mindsets that are exactly the characteristics that we most admire in people who have made important contributions to their respective fields of endeavor—indeed, the creative and productive people that the larger world ultimately refers to as "gifted."

The best way to promote the use of Applied and Created Knowledge is to ensure that special programs place a major focus on providing opportunities to pursue real problems in investigative and creative ways. Real problems differ from other types of assigned problem-solving activities in four basic ways. First, students select the specific problem they want to pursue. This selection may be restricted to an assigned topic or course, but within any general or specific topic area opportunities for personalization of interest creates internal motivation because students have choices based on their own interests. For example, within the general topic area of cognitive science, students might choose to study the effects of a number of variables on memory—age, music, hours of study, testing expectations, and more. A series of general exploratory experiences such as a neuroscientist or field trips to science museums can be used to give students ideas about the choice of a problem in which they might develop a sustained interest (see, for example, Type I Enrichment in the Enrichment Triad Model, Renzulli, 1977).

Second, students are guided in procedures for formulating a hypothesis or research question and the use of authentic investigative methodology such as how practicing historians go about investigating a particular area of study. Developing a hypotheses or research question, selecting a topic for reporting or writing, or designing a science-based community service project ensures that students go beyond just "looking stuff up" and reporting it! It is at this point that teachers need to be able to assist students in finding how-to books and web resources that guide them in finding and focusing on investigable problems. Two types of books, websites, and other resources that teach students about science are helpful in the classroom: content-specific resources and resources based on teaching students science practices. Content-specific resources include texts or Internet resources that teach students about content, such as a website focused on brain anatomy or a book with illustrations about the human body. Science practices include: asking questions and defining problems; developing and using models; planning and carrying out investigations; analyzing and interpreting data; using mathematics and computational thinking; constructing explanations and designing solutions; engaging in argument from evidence; and obtaining, evaluating, and communicating information (NGSS, 2013). A book that teaches students the scientific method might fall into this category.

The third guideline for investigating a real problem is that there is no single predetermined or "correct answer" or prescribed way for conducting a study. There may be some general procedural standards that apply to research in general, but the creativity literature clearly shows us that people who have taken the road less traveled are often the ones who make innovative breakthroughs in their fields of study (Barron, Montuori, & Barron, 1997; Kaufman & Sternberg, 2006; Sternberg, 1988, 2007).[1] The problems that students pursue should also be "fuzzy" ones or open-ended ones, and they should be structured in such a way that it has the potential to change actions, attitudes, or beliefs. Teacher flexibility and a willingness to entertain and respect learning style differences are important conditions at this stage for promoting creativity and the self-efficacy that Bandura (1977) argued are important contributors to independent growth. The teacher (or person who might be recommended as a mentor) must truly

1 John Gurdon, the 2013 winner for the Nobel Prize in medicine, was criticized and given low marks by a high school teacher because "he will not listen and will insist in doing his work in his own way."

be "the-guide-on-the-side" by giving feedback, making suggestions, recommending and helping students secure resources, and providing general support and encouragement. The skills mentioned above for facilitating Analyzed Knowledge activities can be applied here as well. In many ways, the teacher's role at this stage is similar to a college professor's role when guiding a student through a master's or doctoral thesis. This guidance may refer back to both analysis skills and the need to carry our further searches of the Received Knowledge level described above.

The *raison d'être* of the creative/productive person in all societies is to have an impact on one or more intended audiences. That's why writers write, artists paint, builders build, and scientists and engineers produce new products to improve existing work and to make it more effective, efficient, and/or aesthetic. *Their main goal is to make a difference.*

The final guideline for helping students at the Applied and Creative Knowledge level is to assist young people in exploring potential outlets and audiences for their work. This exploration should begin early in the investigative and creative process because it provides motivation to complete and disseminate their work and it is also a good way for students to become familiar with the formats and genres of the areas in which they are working. Opportunities for submitting work for publication or display, both in and especially outside the school, for making presentations and performances to special interest groups, and entering their work into special talent and academic contests and competitions exist in practically all areas of knowledge. These opportunities are highly motivating and provide real-world experiences for teaching students about self-regulation, time management, meeting deadlines, and other executive function skills. One need only examine the legendary success of venues such as Future and Community Problem Solving, the National History Day Competition, the International Science and Engineering Fair, the Invention Convention, and a host of other places to see the role that outlets and audiences play in the creative and productive process.

The right hand side of Figure 3 represents the outcomes of a blended knowledge approach to learning and creative productivity. Increased achievement in the traditional sense is mentioned first because, whether we like it or not, any theory that does not give a prominent place to our overly test-conscience policy makers and the benefits of acceleration in gifted education will be rejected out of hand. But the focus on 21st-century skills has caused policymakers to embrace the importance of including Analyzed Knowledge in the goals of general education, and it is reasonable to assume that they will see the value for considering the importance of blending all three levels discussed here to enhance creative productivity in our high-potential students. It may even be reasonable to hope that they may see some logic in giving students at all levels opportunities to engage in some of the activities that promote Applied and Created Knowledge as well as Received and Analyzed Knowledge. The enjoyment, engagement, and enthusiasm for learning that results from blending all three levels of the learning process may very well turn around the achievement gap and reduce the boredom factor that continues to plague so many students in our schools. But a blended knowledge theory is particularly relevant to our highest achieving students because it represents the modus operandi of gifted contributors in the larger world of knowledge usage and construction.

The theory of knowledge presented here draws upon the wisdom of intellectual founders in the field of epistemology, it takes into account the overstandardization of formal schooling that has taken place over the past several decades, and it recognizes the dramatic changes in learning that are now possible through the use of technology. The theory has special relevance to gifted education because knowledge creation, utilization, and diffusion is what creative and productive people do. Like any other theory, the expectation is that it will generate some research on the parts of interested scholars, and that it will serve a practical purpose of causing us to reexamine our mission, goals, and practices. An important part of the research must focus on longitudinal studies of highly creative and productive adults whose work has made a difference in their chosen fields of endeavor and maybe even changed the world. If we want special programs and services for high potential young people to gain the recognition and support for which we advocate, the best "data" we can put forward is testimony from these people that their gifted programs made a difference that went beyond merely getting good grades, high test scores, and advanced degrees. It must show that we have, indeed, contributed to expanding the reservoir of the world's highly creative and productive people.

CHAPTER 2

The Schoolwide Enrichment Model

This chapter discusses the theory and practices of the SEM, which has been used extensively in schools for decades and is the basis for SEM-Science. The Enrichment Triad Model served as the theoretical and curricular basis for the SEM that is currently implemented in a variety of settings, including gifted programs, enrichment programs, magnet and charter schools, and theme schools. In the SEM, a Talent Pool of approximately 10%–15% of above-average-ability/high-potential students is identified through a variety of measures including: achievement tests, teacher nominations, assessment of potential for creativity and task commitment, as well as alternative pathways of entrance (self-nomination, parent nomination, etc.). High achievement tests and/or IQ test scores automatically include a student in the Talent Pool, enabling those students who are underachieving in their academic schoolwork to be included.

Once students are identified for the Talent Pool, they are eligible for several kinds of services. First, interest and learning style assessments are used with Talent Pool students in the development of a Total Talent Portfolio for each student. Informal and formal methods are used to identify and assess students' interests and to encourage students to further develop and pursue these interests in various ways. Learning style preferences include projects, independent study, teaching games, simulations, peer teaching, computer-assisted instruction, lecture, drill and recitation, and discussion. Second, curriculum compacting and other forms of differentiation and curricular modification are provided to all eligible students when the regular curriculum is adjusted. This elimination or streamlining of curriculum enables above-average students to avoid repetition of previously mastered work and guarantees mastery while simultaneously finding time for more appropriately challenging activities (Reis, Burns, & Renzulli, 1992; Renzulli, Smith, & Reis, 1982). A form, the Compactor (Renzulli & Smith, 1978), is used to document which content areas have been compacted and what alternative work has been substituted. Third, a series of enrichment opportunities organized around the Enrichment Triad Model offers three types of enrichment experiences through various forms of delivery, including enrichment clusters. Types I, II, and III Enrichment are offered to all students; however, Type III Enrichment is usually more appropriate for students of higher levels of ability, interest, and task commitment.

The SEM (Renzulli & Reis, 2014) has three major goals that are designed to challenge and meet the needs of high-potential, high-ability, and gifted students, and at the same time, provide challenging learning experiences for all students. These goals are: (a) to maintain and expand a continuum of special services that will challenge students with demonstrated superior performance or the potential for superior performance in any and all aspects of the school and extracurricular program; (b) to infuse into the general education program a broad range of activities for high-end learning that will challenge all students to perform at advanced levels, and allow teachers to determine which students should be given extended opportunities, resources, and encouragement in particular areas where superior interest and performance are demonstrated; and (c) to preserve and protect the positions of gifted education specialists and any other specialized personnel necessary for carrying out these goals.

The SEM, outlined in Figure 4, has three service delivery components that provide services to students, including the Total Talent Portfolio, curriculum modification and differentiation, and enrichment. These three services are delivered to the regular curriculum, a continuum of special services, and a series of enrichment clusters.

The Total Talent Portfolio

In the SEM, teachers help students better understand three dimensions of their learning—their abilities, interests, and learning styles. This information, focusing on their strengths rather than deficits, is compiled in a management form called the "Total Talent Portfolio" that can be subsequently used to make decisions about talent development opportunities in general education classes, enrichment clusters, and/or in the continuum of special services. The major

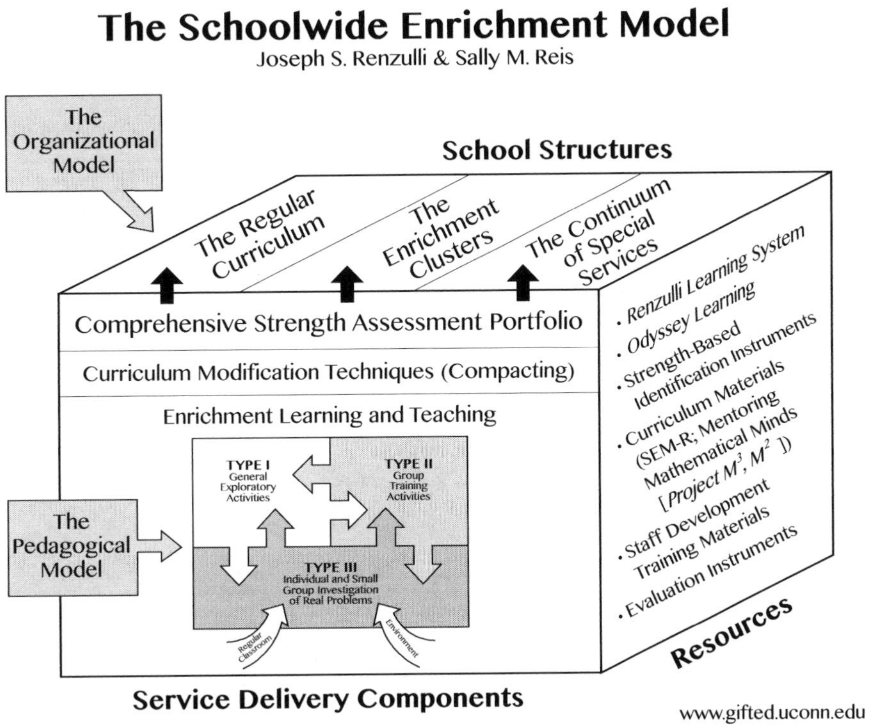

Figure 4. The Schoolwide Enrichment Model.

purposes of the Total Talent Portfolio are: (a) to collect information about students' strengths on a regular basis; (b) to *classify* this information into the general categories of abilities, interests, and learning styles; (c) to periodically *review and analyze* the information in order to make decisions about providing opportunities for enrichment experiences in the general education classroom, the enrichment clusters, and the continuum of special services; and (d) to use this information to make decisions about acceleration and enrichment in school and in later educational, personal, and career decisions. This expanded approach to identifying talent potentials is essential if we are to make genuine efforts to include a broader, more diverse group of students in enrichment programs. This approach is also consistent with the more flexible conception of *developing* gifts and talents that has been a cornerstone of the SEM, addressing concerns for promoting more equity in special programs. More explanation regarding the use of the Total Talent Portfolio in science will be provided in Chapter 3.

Curriculum Modification and Differentiation Techniques

The second service delivery component of the SEM is a series of curriculum modification techniques that can: (a) adjust levels of required learning so that all students are challenged, (b) increase the number of in-depth learning experiences, and (c) introduce various types of enrichment into regular curricular experiences. The procedures that are used to carry out curriculum modification include curriculum differentiation strategies, such as curriculum compacting and increased use of greater depth into regular curricular material (Reis et al., 1993; Renzulli, 1994). Curriculum compacting is an instructional differentiation technique designed to make appropriate curricular adjustments for students in any curricular area and at any grade level through (a) defining the goals and outcomes of a particular unit or segment of instruction, (b) determining and documenting which students already have mastered most or all of a specified set of learning outcomes, and (c) providing replacement strategies for material already mastered through the use of instructional options that enable a more challenging and productive use of the student's time. An example of how compacting is used is best represented in the form "The Compactor," which serves as both an organizational and record-keeping tool (see Figure 5). Teachers should fill out one compactor form per student, or one form for a group of students with similar curricular strengths. Completed Compactors should be kept in students' academic files, and updated on a regular basis. The form can also be used for small groups of students who are working at approximately the same level (e.g., a reading or math group). The Compactor is divided into three sections:

- The first column should include information on learning objectives and student strengths in those areas. Teachers should list the objectives for a particular unit of study, followed by data on students' proficiency in those objectives, including test scores, behavioral profiles, and past academic records.
- In the second column, teachers should detail the assessment tools or procedures they select, along with test results. The pretest instruments can be formal measures, such as pencil and paper tests, or informal measures, such as performance assessments based on observations of class participation and written assignments.
- Column three is used to record information about acceleration or enrichment options; in determining these options, teachers must be aware of students' individual interests and learning styles. We should never

Individual Educational Programming Guide
The Compactor

Prepared by Joseph S. Renzulli
Linda M. Smith

Name: Age: Teacher(s):

School: Grade: Parent(s):

Individual Conference Dates and Persons Participating in Planning of IEP

Curriculum Areas to Be Considered for Compacting Provide a brief description of basic material to be covered during this marking period and the assessment information or evidence that suggests the need for compacting.	**Procedures for Compacting Basic Material** Describe activities that will be used to guarantee proficiency in basic curricular areas.	**Acceleration and/or Enrichment Activities** Describe activities that will be used to provide advanced-level learning experiences in each area of the regular curriculum.

❑ Check here if additional information is recorded on the reverse side.

Figure 5. The Compactor.

simply replace compacted regular curriculum work with more and harder, advanced material that is solely determined by the teacher; instead, students' interests should be considered. If for example, a student loves working on science fair projects, that option may be used to replace material that has been compacted from the regular curriculum. We should also be careful to help monitor the challenge level of the material that is being substituted. We want students to understand the nature of effort and challenge, and we must ensure that we are not simply replacing the compacted material with basic reading or work that is too easy. We should also consider the compatibility of student interests and learning styles when we replace the work that has been compacted.

Enrichment Learning and Teaching

The third service delivery component of the SEM, based on the Enrichment Triad Model, is enrichment learning and teaching that has roots in the ideas of a small but influential number of philosophers, theorists, and researchers such as Jean Piaget (1975), Jerome Bruner (1960, 1966), and John Dewey (1913, 1916). The work of these theorists coupled with our own research and program development activities has given rise to the concept we call *enrichment learning and teaching*. The best way to define this concept is in terms of the following four principles (Renzulli, 1994):

1. Each learner is unique, and therefore, all learning experiences must be examined in ways that take into account the abilities, interests, and learning styles of the individual.
2. Learning is more effective when students enjoy what they are doing, and therefore, learning experiences should be constructed and assessed with as much concern for enjoyment as for other goals.
3. Learning is more meaningful and enjoyable when content (i.e., knowledge) and process (i.e., thinking skills, methods of inquiry) are learned within the context of a real and present problem; therefore, attention should be given to opportunities to personalize student choice in problem selection, the relevance of the problem for individual students at the time the problem is being addressed, and authentic strategies for addressing the problem.
4. Some formal instruction may be used in enrichment learning and teaching, but a major goal of this approach to learning is to enhance

knowledge and thinking skill acquisition that is gained through formal instruction with applications of knowledge and skills that result from students' own construction of meaning.

The ultimate goal of learning guided by these principles is to replace dependent and passive learning with independence and engaged learning. Although all but the most conservative educators will agree with these principles, much controversy exists about how these (or similar) principles might be applied in everyday school situations. A danger also exists that these principles might be viewed as yet another idealized list of glittering generalities that cannot be manifested easily in schools that are entrenched in the deductive model of learning. Developing a school program based on these principles is not an easy task. Over the years, however, we have achieved success by gaining faculty, administrative, and parental consensus on a small number of easy-to-understand concepts and related services, and by providing resources and training related to each concept and service delivery procedure. Numerous research studies and field tests in schools with widely varying demographics have been carried out and are summarized in Renzulli and Reis (1994). These studies and field tests provided opportunities for the development of large amounts of practical know-how that are readily available for schools that would like to implement the SEM. They also have shown that the SEM can be implemented in a wide variety of settings with various populations of students including high-ability students with learning disabilities and high-ability students who underachieve in school.

School Structures of SEM

The Regular Curriculum

The regular curriculum consists of everything that is a part of the predetermined goals, schedules, learning outcomes, and delivery systems of the school. The regular curriculum might be traditional, innovative, or in the process of transition, but its predominant feature is that authoritative forces (i.e., policy makers, school councils, textbook adoption committees, state regulators) have determined that the regular curriculum should be the "centerpiece" of student learning. Application of the SEM influences the regular curriculum in the differentiation of the challenge level of required material using curriculum compacting and the enrichment recommended in the Enrichment Triad Model (Renzulli, 1977) integrated in regular curriculum activities. Although our goal in the SEM is to influence rather than replace the regular curriculum, the application of certain SEM components and related staff development activities has resulted in substantial changes in both the content and instructional processes of the entire regular curriculum.

Enrichment Clusters

The enrichment clusters, a second component of the SEM, are nongraded groups of students who share common interests and who come together during specially designated time blocks during school to work with an adult who shares their interests and who has some degree of advanced knowledge and expertise in the area. The enrichment clusters usually meet for a block of time weekly during a semester. All students complete an interest inventory developed to assess their interests, and an enrichment team of parents and teachers tally all of the major families of interests. Adults from the faculty, staff, parents, and community are recruited to facilitate enrichment clusters based on these interests, such as creative writing, drawing, sculpting, archeology, and other areas. Training is provided to the facilitators who agree to offer the clusters, and a brochure is developed and sent to all parents and students that discusses student interests and choices of enrichment clusters. Students select their top three choices for the clusters and scheduling is completed to place all children into their first, or in some cases, second choice. Like extracurricular activities and programs such as 4-H and Junior Achievement, the main rationale for participation in one or more clusters is that *students and teachers want to be there.* All teachers (including music, art, physical education, etc.) are involved in teaching the clusters, and their involvement in any particular cluster is based on the same type of interest assessment that is used for students in selecting clusters of choice.

The model for learning used with enrichment clusters is based on an inductive approach to solving real-world problems through the development of authentic products and services using the Enrichment Triad Model to create a learning situation with the use of specific methods and the development of higher order thinking skills, authentically applied to creative and productive situations. Enrichment clusters promote real-world problem solving, focusing on the belief that "*every child is special if we create conditions in which that child can be a specialist within a specialty group*" (Renzulli, 1994, p. 70).

Enrichment clusters are organized around various characteristics of differentiated programming for gifted students on which the Enrichment Triad Model (Renzulli, 1977) was originally based, including the use of major disciplines, interdisciplinary themes, or cross-disciplinary topics (e.g., a theatrical/television production group that includes actors, writers, technical specialists, costume designers). The clusters are modeled after the ways in which knowledge utilization, thinking skills, and interpersonal relations take place in the real world. Thus, all work is directed toward the production of a product or service. Cluster facilitators do not prepare a detailed set of lesson plans or unit plans in advance; rather, direction is provided by three key questions addressed in the cluster by the facilitator and the students:

1. What do people with an interest in this area (e.g., film making) do?
2. What knowledge, materials, and other resources do they need to do it in an excellent and authentic way?
3. In what ways can the product or service be used to have an impact on an intended audience?

Enrichment clusters incorporate the use of advanced content, providing students with information about particular fields of knowledge. The methods used within a field are also considered advanced content by Renzulli (1988), involving the use of knowledge of the structures and tools of fields, as well as knowledge about the methodology of particular fields. Enrichment clusters are not intended to be the total program for talent development in a school, or to replace existing programs for talented youth. Rather, they are one component of the SEM that can stimulate interests and develop talent in the entire school population. They can also serve as staff development opportunities as they provide teachers with an opportunity to participate in enrichment teaching, and subsequently to analyze and compare this type of teaching with traditional methods of instruction. In this regard, the model promotes a spillover effect by encouraging teachers to become better talent scouts and talent developers, and to apply enrichment techniques to general education classroom situations.

The Continuum of Special Services

A broad range of special services is the third school structure targeted by the model. Although the enrichment clusters and the SEM-based modifications of the regular curriculum provide a broad range of services to meet individual needs, a program for total talent development still requires supplementary services that challenge our most academically talented young people who are capable of working at the highest levels. These services, which cannot ordinarily be provided in enrichment clusters or the regular curriculum, typically include: individual or small-group counseling, acceleration, direct assistance in facilitating advanced-level work, arranging for mentorships with faculty members or community persons, and making other types of connections between students, their families, and out-of-school persons, resources, and agencies.

Direct assistance also involves setting up and promoting student, faculty, and parental involvement in special programs such as Future Problem Solving, Odyssey of the Mind, the Model United Nations program, and state and national essay competitions, mathematics, art, and history contests. Another type of direct assistance consists of arranging out-of-school involvement for individual students in summer programs, on-campus courses, special schools, theatrical groups, scientific expeditions, and apprenticeships at places where advanced-level learning opportunities are available. Provision of these services is one of the responsibilities of the schoolwide enrichment teaching specialist or an enrichment team of teachers and parents who work together to provide options for advanced learning. Most schoolwide enrichment teaching specialists spend 2 days a week in a resource capacity to the faculty and 3 days providing direct services to students.

Summary

There may never have been a time when so much need has existed to develop students' talents in science and other STEM subjects in American schools. Among developed nations, the United States fares rather poorly on international STEM tests such as the PISA or TIMSS, and science education has been a focus of the current Obama administration through such initiatives as Race to the Top. What form should this science education take? How do teachers inspire students with a passion for learning in science and ensure that our most talented students consider careers in the field? It all begins with knowing the students, and so SEM-Science starts with the Total Talent Portfolio in Science.

CHAPTER 3

The Total Talent Portfolio in Science

Similar to the SEM, the SEM-Science is concerned with the nurturing of the child's learning characteristics and how these characteristics may be considered to develop his or her talent; however, now the focus is on developing talents in science. School personnel who organize science activities must first understand their students, for it is when children are interested in appropriately challenging and interesting activities that they will learn. Many teachers will administer an interest survey at the beginning of the school year to understand their classroom interest. This is an effective and established practice and represents one component of the SEM's Total Talent Portfolio in Science (TTP-Science), which begins with a profiler activity that documents students' learning characteristics. Specifically, the TTP-Science is used to assess students' interests, abilities, expression styles, and learning styles in the field of science. Although many interest surveys are readily available on the Internet, and some of these are even available for science, it is preferable to use a method that collects a broader spectrum of information when documenting students' profiles in these multiple areas.

The TTP has been an established part of the SEM since its inception; however this text extends both the model and the TTP to collect information on students that will allow instruction to be tailored individually to the student *in science*. Therefore, the TTP-Science will vary somewhat from the original version, as instruction in the science classroom favors methods that are suited to the domain of science. These methods are used by practitioners in the field and endorsed by leading organizations such as the National Academies of Science

(NAS) and the National Science Teachers' Association (NSTA)—they include inquiry-based investigations, structured classroom discussions, and more.

Similar to the Total Talent Portfolio in the general SEM, the information in the TTP-Science is first collected and classified into abilities, interests, expression styles, and learning styles, and then this information is used to plan instructional activities and program placement. Information is periodically reviewed and updated, particularly as new interests and abilities emerge. As always, the focus should be on children's strengths, not their deficits. Also, in terms of the larger SEM structure, students' TTP-Science may also be used for program placement. For example, if a group of students are known to be keen on photography and an enrichment cluster is forming to explore this topic, students may be suggested for the cluster. Of course, in the truest sense of the model, the placement is a negotiation between the teacher and the student. Other types of placement that may be guided by students' portfolios include decisions regarding acceleration, afterschool clubs, advanced classes, and more. Parents and older students may be interested in using information in the TTP-Science for career guidance.

The collection of such a broad spectrum of information concerning a student's interests, abilities, expression styles, and learning styles allows for the consideration of the child as a whole. Rather than seeing the child as the product of a small collection of learning deficits, teachers are encouraged to view him or her as possessing a larger, wider set of interests and abilities that may be nurtured and developed.

Getting Started With the Total Talent Portfolio in Science

How does a teacher go about collecting the information required for the TTP-Science? In essence, the Portfolio is a vehicle for collecting the types of information described above. Figure 6 demonstrates the types of information from each of the categories of information: abilities, interests, expression styles, and learning styles.

It is important to consider how each of these areas apply to science, and how each area should be assessed.

Abilities	Interest Areas	Instructional Style Preferences	Expression Style Preferences
Science Content ◆ Tests ▪ Standardized ▪ Teacher-Made ▪ Textbook-Provided ◆ Course Grades **Science Skills** ◆ Performance Assessments ◆ Product Evaluation	**Biology** ◆ Animals ◆ Plants and Fungi ◆ Microorganisms **Physical Science** ◆ Electricity ◆ Force and Motion ◆ Heat and Energy **Chemistry** ◆ Periodic Table of Elements ◆ Chemical Bonds ◆ Phases of Matter ◆ Reactions ◆ Chemical Equations **Astronomy** ◆ Galaxies ◆ Solar Systems ◆ Stars ◆ Planets ◆ Moons ◆ Comets, Asteroids ◆ Origins of the Universe ◆ Extraterrestrial Life **Earth Science** ◆ Geology ◆ Soil ◆ Oceanography ◆ Weather/Climate ◆ Water Cycle **Dispositions** Teacher Ratings (e.g., SRBCSS)	◆ Listening ◆ Discussing ◆ Reading ◆ Investigating ◆ Working With Technology	◆ Written ◆ Verbal/ Discussion ◆ Technology ◆ Manipulative ◆ Models ◆ Art

Figure 6. Total Talent Portfolio in Science.

Abilities

Assessment of a student's abilities in science is concerned with his or her aptitudes and achievements, and specifically, aptitudes and achievements in content knowledge and skills. Aptitude refers to a student's potential ability to accomplish something, whereas achievement refers to a student's actual accomplishments in the area. For example, a student may have aptitude in mathematics but may not apply himself; consequently, his achievement demonstrated through grades may be poor.

To assess students' achievement and aptitude in science content knowledge, as in other subject areas, teachers have traditionally used a number of instruments, including standardized science tests (such as a state-based science assessment that many states use), teacher-made tests, or tests provided by commercially available materials (e.g., "textbook tests"). Course grades are also a traditional assessment in the area of content knowledge. Teachers may also simply ask students how they rate themselves in science compared with other areas.

Students' science process skills should also be assessed. Basic science process skills include simple skills such as observing, inferring, measuring, communicating, classifying, and predicting (Lancour, 2008; Padilla, 1990). Integrated process skills are more complex and include controlling and defining variables operationally, formulating hypotheses, carrying out experiments, organizing and interpreting data to draw conclusions, and formulating models (Lancour, 2008; Padilla, 1990).

To measure students' aptitude for using basic and integrated science skills, performance assessments may be used. One such example of this type of performance assessment is the Diet Cola Test (Fowler, 1990), which has two standard forms and is reprinted with permission here in Handout 1. (All handouts are available electronically on the book's website at http://www.prufrock.com/Assets/ClientPages/SEM_Science.aspx and in reproducible form at the end of each chapter.) In this assessment, students are asked to design a fair test of the question, "How would you do a fair test of this question: Are bees attracted to diet cola?" Students write about how they would design their investigations, and instructors may rate them using the scoring guide in Handout 2. Here, instructors score the response based on 15 criteria, included in the scoring guide. These 15 criteria include the wording of the problem or question, plans to repeat testing, and plans to control variables. Scores for each item range from 0–2, depending on the level of detail included (Adams & Callahan, 1995), and points are totaled to provide the instructor with an overall general score. Using this assessment will especially provide teachers with a deeper understanding of how students are able to apply integrated science skills such as developing hypotheses, controlling variables, and more.

Another way to understand students' abilities in science and engineering is by rating them on the NGSS Cross-Cutting Practices (NGSS Lead States, 2013). These eight practices include:

1. Asking questions (for science) and defining problems (for engineering).
2. Developing and using models.
3. Planning and carrying out investigations.
4. Analyzing and interpreting data.
5. Using mathematics and computational thinking.
6. Constructing explanations (for science) and designing solutions (for engineering).
7. Engaging in argument from evidence.
8. Obtaining, evaluating, and communicating information (NGSS Lead States, 2013, Appendix F).

Handout 3 separates each of these practices and allows the teacher to rate individual students on a scale of 0–4. These scores are not meant to be summed; however, the scale will provide a good understanding of students' strengths and weaknesses in each of the areas.

Interest Areas

A second important component of the TTP is student interest in subdomains within science, including biology, physical science, chemistry, astronomy, Earth science, and engineering. One way to gauge interest levels in these areas in science is to administer the Student Interest Survey for SEM-Science, presented in Handout 4. A convenient scoring guide is included in Handout 5. Again, caution must be applied when interpreting these scores, for they are meant to be general indications of a student's interest in each of the areas, and the scores should be interpreted with additional information, such as answers to the following questions (included in the scoring guide):

- What does the student like to talk about in science? What lights him or her up?
- Does the student have a collection of any type? For example, does the student have a rock collection?
- What types of books, magazines, or articles does the student like to read in science?

- What do the student's parents tell you about the child's interests in science?

In addition to students' interest in individual areas within science, we must consider students' dispositions toward science in general. By dispositions, we mean whether the student likes science, thinks scientifically, and is able to use the practices of science to engage with topics. These dispositions are increasingly emphasized by the bodies that govern science education, including the National Research Council (Michaels, Shouse, & Schweingruber, 2008), which identifies the ability to participate productively in science as one of four major strands that must be addressed in the classroom. One way to document students' dispositions in science is through the use of a survey or inventory completed by the teacher, such as the Scales for Rating the Behavioral Characteristics of Superior Student (SRBCSS; Renzulli et al., 2013). Although this survey may be completed for students in a number of areas, including mathematics, creativity, reading, learning characteristics, and more, the science questions are most relevant to the current discussion. Teachers are asked to rate the student on seven questions using a scale ranging from Never to Always and these seven questions primarily cover students' dispositions toward science. These seven questions are provided in Handout 6.

Instructional Styles

It is important to take into account students' instructional style preferences, or the way that they prefer to learn content or skills during a lesson. Learning is optimized when students have an opportunity, at least sometimes, to learn through a preferred method. Instructional styles frequently found in science include lecture, reading, discussion, investigations and experiments, and working with technology. Not so coincidentally, these learning styles mirror the practices used by scientists in the field, and they are increasingly encouraged by a robust body of research as best practices for the science classroom (Michaels et al., 2008). Instructional style preferences in science may be assessed using the SEM Science Instructional Styles Inventory, provided in Handout 7. The inventory may be scored using the Scoring Sheet in Handout 8.

Lecture. A widely used approach to teaching almost any subject for many decades has been the lecture format. Sometimes classified as "sage on the stage," teachers may utilize this approach because they were taught in this manner. Efficient for delivering some types of content information, the lecture format is appropriate in certain circumstances and may actually be preferred by some children. However, overuse of this type of format may lead to passive learning and a lack of opportunity for children to practice or apply knowledge or skills.

Reading. Books, chapters, and articles are still used in today's classrooms to interest science students. Trade books, or books that describe scientific phenomena to children, abound at all age and reading levels. We recommend that teachers still acquire these and keep them in the classroom, both to promote students' interests in topics with which they may not be familiar and to serve as aides during investigations. The difference between classrooms now and classrooms 30 years ago is that now teachers frequently have the option to collect electronic books on portable devices so that students may more easily access them. Many of these books even have interactive features that make them more engaging to children.

Discussion. Discussion has become a popular and important way to teach in science, and by discussion we mean a structured approach or set of "talk moves" that allows students to address not only the teacher, but each other in order to build upon or evaluate ideas. Six specific talk moves that allow for structured discussion include revoicing what a student said, asking students to state someone else's reasoning, asking them to apply their own reasoning to someone else's reasoning, prompting students for further participation, asking students to explicate their reasoning, and using wait time before calling on students to answer questions (Chapin, O'Connor, & Anderson, 2003).

In addition to talk moves, teachers may utilize different discussion formats to encourage productive discussion in the classroom. These different formats include partner sharing, collaborative small-group work, student presentations, and whole-classroom discussions. Frequently these types of formats help students build upon their own ideas, provide them with necessary think time, and also mimic the way scientific practitioners communicate in the real world (Michael et al., 2008).

Investigations and experiments. Science investigations are called out in the Next Generation Science Standards as an important element of scientific practices. For decades, educators used the term *inquiry* to refer to investigations, but the term was used in so many different ways that the definition became muddled. Theorists and educators are now placing the process of inquiry within a broader context of science and engineering practices that may be used to conduct science in a meaningful way. These practices include: asking questions and defining problems; developing and using models; planning and carrying out investigations; analyzing and interpreting data; using mathematics and computational thinking; constructing explanations and designing solutions; engaging in argument from evidence; and obtaining, evaluating, and communicating information (NGSS Lead States, 2013).

The term *experiment* refers to a specific type of investigation, one in which variables are defined and carefully controlled in order to test a hypothesis (Michaels et al., 2013). All experiments are therefore investigations, but investigations may not be experiments. For example, an investigation may consist of students observing and sketching the wings of a butterfly to try to determine similarities and differences. However, if students investigated the effect of light on the wings of a butterfly to test the hypothesis that light darkened the wings' color, they would be conducting an experiment. In both cases, students are investigating a phenomenon so both are considered investigations, but only the second case involves an experiment.

Fieldwork is frequently a component of investigations or experiments; it involves the collection of data outside of the classroom. Fieldwork doesn't have to cost a lot of money or be difficult—it could simply consist of having students examine the type of insects in a playground or count the number of students buying lunch in the cafeteria. Fieldwork can also be artificially constructed, such as when a teacher creates an archaeological "dig" for her students by planting artifacts in a plot of land near the school for her students to dig up. Of course, some fieldwork may be more complex, such as when a classroom visits an environmental studies center to collect and record salinity and turbidity information on a local estuary.

Another type of investigation may not at first appear to be an actual investigation. When students build models, they are doing an investigation of sorts. They are assembling parts into a whole that is meant to resemble something that is either larger or more abstract than the model. The purpose of building a model is so that students may investigate the characteristics of the original item, and so the nature of model-building is investigatory.

Technology and simulations. Students may favor learning through technology over the traditional method. Here, we mean learning through the use of a computer, a smart device such as a phone or tablet, or the use of other types of technology such as robotics.

One type of specialized activity that frequently makes use of technology is the simulation. Students favor simulations as an instructional preference because they can be extremely interactive and engaging, and they usually involve the use of technology to immerse the student in the situation. Simulations may take the form of recreating the experience for the student—for example, a virtual frog dissection may allow students to learn about the internal organs of the frog without having to deal with harsh chemicals or the complex reality of sacrificing animals for the purpose. Simulations may also place students in situations that may not be possible without technology. For example, simulations that allow students to fly through the solar system or "walk" on another planet allow students to explore their universe in unique and exciting ways that they probably will never do in real life. A third type of simulation takes the form of a game that challenges students to complete a goal—for example, a simulation that requires students to colonize a virtual Mars by using certain resources.

Expression Styles

Let's imagine that the lesson is over and the student is about to demonstrate the results of learning. How does he or she prefer to do so? Is it through writing or orally? Is it through a model or artistically? These expression styles are important to consider, because students must be allowed, at least at times, to work within their preferred expression style if they are to continue to be engaged with learning. Of course, it is not usually possible to allow all students to express themselves exclusively through their preferred styles, but by understanding the general expression styles of students in your classroom, and by varying these styles throughout your lessons, students may be allowed to work at least sometimes in their preferred style. The expression styles most frequently used in science include writing, technology, discussions, making a model, and especially hands-on laboratory projects and preparing for a science fair.

Written. Teachers most frequently use written reports in their classrooms, and there are many times in science when written work is necessary and desirable. For example, asking students to write in science journals has been shown to be effective at advancing learning in the domain.

Verbal/Discussion. Verbal or oral expression styles allow students either to express their ideas quickly so that teachers can determine their level of understanding or in a more formal way (such as an oral report before the class). Verbal may also include debate or discussion in the classroom.

Technology. Written and oral expression have been with us for millennia, but expression aided by technology is a more recent invention. Here, we are not referring to simply typing up a written report; rather, we are referring to using presentation software such as PowerPoint, Prezi, Glogster, and more—software that allows students to produce complex products in terms of combining text, images, sounds, and movement. We are also referring to the production of podcasts, websites, blogs, wikis, and such.

Manipulative. Manipulative products are produced by the hands. In science, such manipulation is especially desirable as students explore their world kinesthetically. Examples of manipulative products in science might include elaborate and formal products, such as an invention built for an Invention Convention, a science fair board, or a robot entered into a robotics competition. However, they might also include more informal products, such as when a student combines two chemicals to study the reaction.

Models. Modeling is different from producing manipulative products, because a model captures attributes inherent to its target. For example, a model car may capture the mechanical parts of the real thing in miniature.

Allowing students to construct models is an appropriate and effective way to enable them to understand complex systems. Modeling is about taking data or information and organizing it in such a way as to be able to make sense of it. Most of us understand that when students build a miniature replica of the Earth or a car engine, they are constructing models. However, graphs of data, including line and bar charts, pie charts, and more are also models because through these students organize data into some type of representational form. Students' abilities and takeaways from the modeling experience grow increasingly more complex as they develop. For example, early elementary students may focus on building simple, descriptive models, such as stems of flowers that represent the height of the flower. By the middle of elementary school, they are able to use these visual representations to make comparisons—to see similarities and differences, to notice patterns, and to use mathematics such as ratios to draw conclusions. By the end of elementary school, students are able to or may focus on many more attributes of the target (e.g., height, width, weight, color) and are able to use evidence from something other than the model itself to draw conclusions. For example, if they are graphing the height of flowers and notice that one set of flowers grew taller than another set, they might conclude that the second set received more sunlight. Students at this stage may also attempt to collect data and draw conclusions based on similarities and differences between the item studied (e.g., a plant) and another item (an animal; Lehrer & Schauble, 2006). Models used in this way can be a powerful instructional tool in the science classroom.

Art. We don't usually think of science and art going together, yet for centuries scientists have used artistic expression as a tool to study their environments. For example, Charles Darwin sketched nature incessantly, and his detailed sketches of certain animals in the Galapagos Islands enabled him to see that creatures of the same species exhibited different characteristics on different islands. This observation led directly to the understanding of natural selection, or the idea that organisms mutate over time, and that if a mutation allows an organism to fit best within its particular environment, that organism will be more likely to survive and pass on the gene for the mutation. Eventually, the mutation may become a dominant characteristic within the species, and most or all of the entire species will have evolved to carry the characteristic. From this idea came the Theory of Evolution. Students may use drawing or other forms of artistic expression to study the world around them in the same manner that Charles Darwin did, or they may use art in science as a product of expression. For example, they may imagine and draw a new species or make a collage that depicts the climate, plants, and animals of an ecosystem that they've studied.

Service project. The service project is a more unusual form of expression, yet it is an important one. Many students are drawn to the idea of serving a greater cause, and this cause is frequently in the service of humanity or nature; service projects are natural fits within science because the subjects with which science deals often lend themselves to the betterment of others. For example, students might study the fragile ecosystem of a local pond, find evidence of pollution, investigate the causes, and develop a recovery plan, which they then use to persuade authorities to clean it up. Or they might study the harm that speeding boaters inadvertently bring to manatees in their community's inlets and campaign to install "Slow Down for Manatees" signs in the local waters. Expression styles may be assessed using the instrument in Handout 9 and scored using the handouts in Handout 10.

Implementing the Total Talent Portfolio in Science

One caveat must be mentioned before describing how to implement the Total Talent Portfolio in Science—it is meant to serve as a guide to understanding each student's abilities, interests, and expression styles in the classroom; it is not meant to be used in cases where cut-offs are necessary. For example, it is not meant to be used in determining placement in gifted classes. Rather, it is to help the instructor develop a well-rounded sense of who the student is in order to plan curriculum and guide the student to a greater sense of self-awareness.

An organizational form has been included in Handout 11, which is divided into five sections that correspond to the types of diagnostic information described in this chapter, namely students' abilities in science, interests in science, dispositions in science, preference for instructional styles in science, and preference for expression styles in science. Teachers may either print the form and use it in students' portfolios or use the digital version in their electronic portfolios. It is recommended that the instruments in the chapter be administered at the start of the school year and that assessment information be entered onto this form. A description summary has been included as the last component on the form to provide a convenient way to gain a snapshot of the science student as a whole.

Once this type of diagnostic information is obtained, students may be viewed as a complex collection of abilities, interests, and preferences so that learning may be delivered in a more targeted fashion. For example, if most of the class is interested in rock collecting, a unit of instruction may be planned around this topic. Differentiation also provides another way to use the handout to target instruction. For example, the opportunity may present itself for the class to study oceans, and if most of the students show a high level of interest in oceanography but have different instructional preferences, they may be placed in groups organized by these preferences, mastering the same objectives through different ways.

Name: Date:

HANDOUT 1

The Diet Cola Investigation

Directions:

How would you do a fair test of this question?

"Are bees attracted to Diet Cola?" (In other words, do bees like Diet Cola?) Tell how you would test this question. Be as scientific as you can as you write about your test. Write down the steps you would take to find out if bees like Diet Cola.

Note. From "The diet cola test" (pp. 32–34) by M. Fowler, 1990, *Science Scope, 13*(4). Reprinted with permission.

Student Name: Date:

HANDOUT 2

Fowler Science Process Skills Assessment—Scoring Sheet

Directions: Score one point on student paper for each item incorporated into design. Score two points if more than one subitem is listed for a specific item.

		Score
plans to practice SAFETY		
states PROBLEM or QUESTION		
PREDICTS outcome or HYPOTHESIZES		
lists more than 3 steps		
arranges steps in SEQUENTIAL order		
lists MATERIALS needed		
plans to REPEAT TESTING and tells reason		
other items listed by student but not on list		
DEFINES the terms of the experiment: "attacted to""likes""bees""Diet Cola"	DEFINES the terms of the experiment: "attracted to""likes""earthworms""light"	
plans to OBSERVE		
plans to MEASURE: (e.g., linear distance between bees, and/or cola, number of bees, time involved)	plans to MEASURE: (e.g., linear distance between worms, and/or light, number of worms, time involved, amount of light)	
plans DATA COLLECTION: graph or table; note taking; labels		
states plan for INTERPRETING DATA: comparing data; looking for patterns in data; in terms of definitions used; in terms of previously known information		
states plan for making CONCLUSION BASED ON DATA: (e.g., time to notice drinks; bees may not be hungry; distances to sodas are equal; time involved for two samles is equal; temperature, light, wind, etc., are equal)	states plan for making CONCLUSION BASED ON DATA: (e.g., time to notice light; distances to light and shade are equal; time involved for two samples is equal; temperature, wind, etc., are equal)	
Plans to CONTROL VARIABLES: (e.g., bees not hungry, bees choose diet or regular soda; distances set equally; amounts of soda equal; number of bees tested are equal; temperature, light, wind, etc., are equal)	Plans to CONTROL VARIABLES: (e.g., worms choose dark or light; distances set equally; number of worms tested are equal; time involved is equal; temperature, wind, etc., are equal)	
	Total:	______/30 points

Note. From "The diet cola test" (pp. 32–34) by M. Fowler, 1990, *Science Scope, 13*(4). Reprinted with permission.

Student Name: Date:

HANDOUT 3

Teacher Rating Scale for NGSS Cross-Cutting Practices

Directions: Rate the student's ability to do the following:

0—Does Not Demonstrate Behavior

1—Demonstrates Behavior, but Struggles With Task

2—Demonstrates Behavior, but Meets Expectations and Is Able to Complete the Task Adequately

3—Demonstrates Behavior, and Exceeds Expectations

	0	1	2	3
Asks questions.				
Defines problems.				
Plans and carries out investigations.				
Analyzes and interprets data.				
Uses mathematics and computational thinking.				
Constructs explanations.				
Designs solutions.				
Engages in argument from evidence.				
Obtains and evaluates information.				
Communicates information.				

Name: Date:

HANDOUT 4

Student Interest Survey for SEM-Science

Directions: Think about your interests in science. Most kids your age have one or more interests in science. Check the category that tells how much you like or dislike these things.

	Really Dislike	Dislike	Not Sure	Like	Really Like
1. Learning about plants.					
2. Learning about animals.					
3. Learning about living things that you can see under a microscope.					
4. Learning about electricity.					
5. Learning about how things move.					
6. Learning about how things heat up or cool down.					
7. Learning about what kinds of matter goes into making up things.					
8. Learning about how you can change a solid into a liquid (for example, ice into water).					
9. Combining different kinds of chemicals to see what happens.					
10. Learning about things in the sky (for example, planets and stars).					
11. Learning about how the universe was formed.					
12. Learning about how life might exist on other planets.					
13. Learning about rocks.					
14. Learning about how weather happens.					
15. Learning about the oceans.					
16. Learning about how machinery works.					
17. Learning about how to build something.					
18. Learning about how to make a model.					

Student Name: Date:

HANDOUT 5

Scoring Key for SEM-Science Interest Survey

Directions:

1. Assign point values in the table below to each question as follows:
   Really Like—5
   Like—4
   Not Sure—3
   Dislike—2
   Really Dislike—1

2. Total the numbers for each interest area in science. Lower scores indicate less interest, and higher scores indicate more interest.

3. Record the totals for each interest area in the last rows of the table.

4. Answer the questions below the table for further consideration.

Question Number	Interest Area	Score (1–5)
1	Biology	
2	Biology	
3	Biology	
	Total for Biology:	
4	Physics	
5	Physics	
6	Physics	
	Total for Physics:	
7	Chemistry	
8	Chemistry	
9	Chemistry	
	Total for Chemistry:	
10	Astronomy	
11	Astronomy	
12	Astronomy	
	Total for Astronomy:	
13	Earth Science	
14	Earth Science	
15	Earth Science	
	Total for Earth Science:	

Student Name: Date:

HANDOUT 5, CONTINUED

Question Number	Interest Area	Score (1–5)
16	Engineering	
17	Engineering	
18	Engineering	
	Total for Engineering:	
	Totals for Each Interest Area	
	Biology	
	Physics	
	Chemistry	
	Astronomy	
	Earth Science	
	Engineering	

5. What does the student like to talk about in science? What lights him or her up?

___

___

___

6. Does the student have a collection of any type? For example, does the student have a rock collection?

___

___

___

7. What types of books, magazines, or articles does the student like to read in science?

___

___

___

8. What do the student's parents tell you about the child's interests in science?

___

___

___

Student Name: Date:

HANDOUT 6

Scales for Rating the Behavioral Characteristics of Superior Students—Science Characteristics

The student . . .	Never	Very Rarely	Rarely	Occasionally	Frequently	Always
demonstrates curiosity about scientific processes.						
demonstrates creative thinking about scientific debates and issues.						
demonstrates enthusiasm in discussion of scientific topics.						
is curious about why things are as they are.						
reads about science topics in his or her free time.						
clearly articulates data interpretation.						
Add Column Total						
Multiply by Weight	1	2	3	4	5	6
Add Weighted Column Totals	+	+	+	+	+	+
Scale Total						________/36

Name: Date:

HANDOUT 7

SEM-Science Instructional Styles Inventory

Directions: Think about the ways you like to learn in science class. Read each sentence and think about whether it describes an activity that you would like to do in school. Choose the answer that shows how much you like or dislike a certain kind of learning activity in science.

	Really Dislike	Dislike	Not Sure	Like	Really Like
1. Listen to the teacher explain something in science class.					
2. Read about a topic in science.					
3. Discuss something related to science in your class.					
4. Do a science investigation or a science experiment where you try to do a fair test of something.					
5. Build a model in science class.					
6. Work on the computer in science.					
7. Read an article or magazine in science.					
8. Play an interactive game on the computer in science.					
9. Talk about science with a partner in science class.					
10. Try to experience something on the computer that you could not do in real life (for example, fly to the moon).					
11. Listen to the teacher talk about science.					
12. Go outside somewhere to observe or collect something.					
13. Read a book about science.					
14. Participate in a group discussion about something in science.					
15. Listen to an expert explain something in science.					

Student Name: Date:

HANDOUT 8

Scoring Sheet for SEM-Science Instructional Styles Inventory

Directions:

1. For each question, review the student's answer.
2. Assign a number to the answer as follows:
   Really Dislike—1
   Dislike—2
   Not Sure—3
   Like—4
   Really Like—5
3. In the Scoring Table below, enter the number that corresponds to the student's preferred learning style into the white box next to the question number. For example, if a student responds "Really Likes" on Question 1, you would record a 5 in the first column's white box next to Question Number 1.
4. Add the values for each column. These totals will provide an understanding for how much a student likes to do a certain activity. Higher scores mean that the student likes to do the activity more.

Item Number	Listening	Discussing	Reading	Investigating	Working With Technology
1					
2					
3					
4					
5					
6					
7					
8					
9					
10					
11					
12					
13					
14					
15					
Total:					

Name: Date:

HANDOUT 9

SEM-Science Expression Style Inventory

1. When you finish learning about something in science, you usually produce something to express your ideas or tell about what you have learned. Check the top three ways you like to do this.
   - ❑ Write about it.
   - ❑ Discuss it.
   - ❑ Use a computer or other technology to do show what you have learned.
   - ❑ Use your hands to make something.
   - ❑ Make a model of something.
   - ❑ Draw a picture or produce another type of art.

2. Read each item below and decide how much you like creating products or expressing yourself *in science class* in a certain way.

	Really Dislike	Dislike	Not Sure	Like	Really Like
a. Building a model of something that I studied.					
b. Writing a report about what I have learned.					
c. Using the computer to produce a PowerPoint or another type of presentation on what I have learned.					
d. Building something other than a model.					
e. Drawing a picture.					
f. Discussing what I have learned with the class.					
g. Making a diagram about something I learned.					
h. Doing something to help others.					
i. Talking about something I learned in science with a partner in science class.					
j. Doing something to help the environment.					
k. Designing a website or something else on the computer.					
l. Painting a picture.					
m. Writing about an investigation.					
n. Talking about my ideas that I learned in science.					
o. Making a graph or chart about what I learned.					
p. Building an invention.					
q. Writing a story about something I learned in science.					
r. Doing something to help plants or animals.					
s. Filming or editing a video.					
t. Drawing a mural on a wall.					
u. Repairing a machine.					

Student Name: Date:

HANDOUT 10

Scoring Sheet for SEM-Science Expression Styles Inventory—Scoring Directions

Directions:

1. For Question 1, review the student's top three choices. Place a 5 in the columns that he or she selected in the Scoring Table below.
2. For the remainder of the questions, assign a number to the answer as follows:
   Really Dislike—1
   Dislike—2
   Not Sure—3
   Like—4
   Really Like—5

3. In the Scoring Table below, enter the number that corresponds to the student's preferred learning style into the white box next to the question number. For example, if a student responds "Really Likes" on Question 1, you would record a 5 in the first column's white box next to Question Number 1.
4. Add the values for each column. These totals will provide an understanding for how much a student likes to do a certain activity. Higher scores mean that the student prefers to express him- or herself in this way.

Item Number	Written	Verbal/ Discussion	Technology	Manipulative	Models	Art	Service
1.							
2a.							
2b.							
2c.							
2d.							
2e.							
2f.							
2g.							
2h.							
2i.							
2j.							
2k.							

Student Name: Date:

HANDOUT 10, CONTINUED

Item Number	Written	Verbal/ Discussion	Technology	Manipulative	Models	Art	Service
2l.							
2m.							
2n.							
2o.							
2p.							
2q.							
2r.							
2s.							
2t.							
2u.							
Total:							

HANDOUT 11

Schoolwide Enrichment Model Science Portfolio Organizer

Student Name: ____________________

Grade Level: __________ **Teacher:** ____________________

1. **Ability in Science**
   a. Science Content
      1. The student's average science test scores (teacher-made and/or textbook) are in which range (check one): ❑ Low ❑ Middle ❑ High
      2. Standardized test score in science:

         Name of test: ____________________ Percentile scored: __________
      3. Average course report card grade in science: ____________________

   b. Science Skills
      1. Enter score on Diet Cola Test (Handout 1): __________/30 points
         Check a range based on points:

         ❑ 0–7 Low ❑ 8–15 Average ❑ 16–23 Above Average ❑ 24–30 High

         List Particular Strengths (e.g., developing a hypothesis, observing):

         ____

         ____
      2. Product evaluation
         Quality of science fair (Check one): ❑ Outstanding ❑ Good ❑ Average ❑ Poor

         Quality of invention convention (Check one):
         ❑ Outstanding ❑ Good ❑ Average ❑ Poor

         Other: ❑ Outstanding ❑ Good ❑ Average ❑ Poor

2. **Interest Areas in Science**
   a. Enter the student's score from the SEM-Science Interest Survey (Handout 4) for each area below:

      Biology: __________

      Physics: __________

      Chemistry: __________

      Astronomy: __________

Student Name: ______________________ Date: ______________________

HANDOUT 11, CONTINUED

3. **Dispositions in Science**
   a. Enter Total Scale Score for SCRBCSS (Handout 6): ______ out of 36 possible points.
   b. Based on this score and your observations, how would you rate the student's enthusiasm for and engagement in science (check one):

   ❑ Low ❑ Average ❑ Above Average ❑ High

4. **Instructional Style Preferences**
   a. Enter the score from the SEM-Science Instructional Style Inventory (Handout 7) for each area below:

   Listening: ______________________

   Discussing: ______________________

   Reading: ______________________

   Investigating: ______________________

   Working With Technology: ________

5. **Expression Style Preferences**
   a. Enter the score from the SEM-Science Expression Style Inventory (Handout 9) for each area below:

   Writing: ______________________

   Verbal/Discussion: ______________

   Technology: ______________________

   Manipulative: ______________________

   Models: ______________________

   Art: ______________________

Summary:

______________________________________ is a student who normally scores in the _______________ (1.a.1) range on science tests. He/she scored in the ______________ percentile (1.a.2) on a standardized science assessment, and his/her science grades are usually _______________s (1.a.3). The student's process skills are in the __________ range (1.b.1); particular strengths included ____________________ and _______________________ (1.b.1). When he/she does a science fair project or invention convention, the project is generally ____________________ (1.b.2).

Student Name: ______________________ Date: ______________

HANDOUT 11, CONTINUED

The student's primary interest is in ____________________, followed by ______________________ (2.a). His/her enthusiasm for and engagement in science is ____________________ (3.b). The student's most favorite way to learn in science is by ____________________ (4.a) and the least favorite way to learn is by ________________________________ (4.a). When finished, his/her favorite way to demonstrate learning is through an activity involving ___________________________ (4.b); his/her least favorite way to demonstrate learning is through an activity involving _____________________________ (4.b).

Based on this summary, the student would benefit from an activity in science that is focused on ___________________________ (2.a) through ___________________________ (4.a) that allows him/her to demonstrate learning through ____________________________(4.b).

CHAPTER 4

Engaging Students Through Type I Activities in Science

At the heart of the SEM-Science is the Enrichment Triad Model, designed to engage students with learning and inspire their curiosity to learn more. The model exposes students to a wide variety of topics, areas of interest, and fields of study, and teaches them how to apply advanced content and skills to complete a self-selected authentic project. An integral component of the Enrichment Triad Model, Type I activities are the "hooks" for motivating our young scientists, hooks that expose students to the vast world and opportunities embedded within the discipline. It is also the first sequential step that leads to the completion of Type II and Type III activities, which build knowledge and skills and work toward the production of an authentic learning project in science.

In the general SEM structure, Type I activities are focused on providing enriching activities to students across the school. In SEM-Science, teachers who deliver science instruction work together to plan Type I activities that are specifically targeted to the domain of science. These activities could be implemented with all students in a systematic way, or they could be offered to Talent Pool students. Similar to Type I activities in the general SEM, these activities in science have three main purposes:

- To enrich the lives of all students by expanding the scope of experiences not covered by the school.
- To stimulate new interests that might lead to more intensive follow-up activity (Type III) on the part of the individual or small groups of students.

› To give teachers direction for making meaningful decisions about the kinds of Type II Enrichment activities that should be selected for particular groups of students (Renzulli & Reis, 2014, p. 84).

Type I Activities in Science

What does a Type I activity look like in science? How is it the same and how is it different than a Type I in the general SEM? Let's consider an example by imagining a SEM-Science classroom taught by Mrs. D., who is a veteran sixth-grade science teacher eager to expose her students to more science. At the start of the school year, Mrs. D. has spent some time creating profiles for her students using the diagnostic instruments described in Chapter 3. Now that she understands her students' interests in and dispositions toward science, as well as their instructional learning styles and expression preferences, she is ready to plan her curriculum. She has noticed that many of her students share an interest in biology, and so she discusses this fact with her planning team, who decide to kick off the year with a series of Type I activities related to biology. The team consists of four teachers who work together to plan and implement curricula for the entire sixth grade, and after they meet, they decide that they will invite two biologists from the local marine center to come and speak with their classes regarding the estuary, its lifeforms, and problems related to pollution that have developed over the previous decade and now endanger estuary wildlife. They also develop two interest centers, one on infant marine life that reside in the fragile estuary and one on sources of pollution. They collect several videos on the topic as well, and they plan one brief initial investigation by bringing in a container of estuary water containing thousands of tiny marine life forms that students will examine under a microscope. This team has utilized the diagnostic information in students' profiles to plan a curricular unit on marine life, and their multifaceted approach to Type I activities will kick off the unit and ignite children's interest in the topic. Hopefully, students will want to take the topic to the next level, exploring and learning about estuaries and marine life more deeply, and some students may go on to produce a Type III authentic learning project on the topics.

Some of these activities appear similar to Type I activities in the overall SEM: teachers used interest centers, videos, and speakers to promote interest in a topic. However, two essential differences between SEM-Science Type I activities and the general nature of SEM Type I experiences are as follows:

1. Teachers use diagnostic information from the SEM-Science talent portfolio to plan and implement high-interest activities in *science*.
2. A few Type I activities in SEM-Science are included that were not in the general Type I activities, because these activities lend themselves to exploration in science. For example, doing a preliminary investigation as in the microscope example provided above may spark students' interest in a topic and encourage them to continue to explore the topic.

The SEM-Science Planning Team

It is possible for the individual classroom teacher to plan activities in the SEM-Science Model. A teacher might, for example, gather science apps, plan and arrange for speakers and field trips related to science, and develop engaging demonstrations and investigations. However, the old saying that two heads are better than one really does apply here. More people frequently translates into more (and sometimes better) ideas, so how does one go about building a SEM-Science planning team?

The first and most natural possibility is for a teacher to reach out to members of the assigned planning team with whom he or she works. This team often consists of other teachers of the same grade level (e.g., other fifth-grade teachers), or teams may be organized around content areas. If the latter circumstance is the case, science teachers may naturally form the SEM-Science planning team. A third option is to reach out to teachers with an interest and knowledge in science across grade levels. For example, consider who the leaders are in planning and teaching science in first grade, in second grade, and so on.

It is frequently helpful to involve 6–10 members who are not classroom teachers, for they bring additional types of expertise, resources, and contacts to the experience. These members may be found within or outside of the school, and could include:

Within the school:

- administrators,
- counselors,
- psychologists,
- content specialists and coaches,
- resource room specialists,
- support staff, and
- volunteers.

Outside the school:

- scientists,
- lab technicians,
- health-care professionals (e.g., doctors, nurses, dentists),
- business owners,
- museum curators, and
- parents.

These lists are by no means complete, and so any person with an interest in science and with time and energy to donate should be considered. An example of an e-mail that may be used to invite SEM-Science team members has been included in Figure 7.

Considerations for the SEM-Science Team

When the SEM-Science team meets for the first time, participants will need to make a number of key decisions that will shape the outcome of the venture. To guide this first meeting, a suggested agenda has been provided in Figure 8.

The organizer will wish to consider holding the meeting in a convenient location (for most people that will be the school), and refreshments may be provided as a way of thanking volunteers for their time. A welcome and introductions may put members at ease, and it's often helpful to include some type of icebreaker activity. The purpose of SEM-Science should be explained as a way to engage students in the discipline by identifying and then using their particular interests and learning profile to create a challenging and enriching curriculum. The organizer should make clear that the role of the planning team is to guide the process by providing ideas regarding enrichment opportunities and access to resources—people, places, and things—that may be used to this end.

Now the organizer will wish to begin soliciting ideas from team members for resources—people who may be contacted to speak, businesses that might provide either financial support or in-kind donations, locations that might be visited, and more. At this point, the composition of the SEM-Science team becomes either its greatest asset or its greatest liability. If the team is varied in terms of occupations, ages, economic backgrounds, ethnicities, neighborhoods, and more, members will have access to many different types of resources. However, if the team is homogeneous in terms of these things, it may be difficult to develop a comprehensive set of resources and additional members may need to be recruited.

Dear ______________________________,

We are excited to announce that we will be using the Schoolwide Enrichment Model in Science this year at our school. The Schoolwide Enrichment Model has been used successfully for decades at hundreds of schools across the country and internationally, and now we will be applying it to science.

We are assembling individuals with an interest in science to help plan the process, and we hope that you'll consider joining us. As part of the SEM-Science Planning Team, you can make a valuable contribution to students' engagement and learning in science at our school. By donating your time, expertise, and energy, you will be able to help us plan and implement engaging activities for students in grades ______ through ______.

We anticipate that our first meeting will be held on ____________ [date] at ________ [time] in __________________________ [location]. We hope to meet regularly once a ____________ [week, month] for the remainder of the school year.

Please let us know if you would be interested in serving on the SEM-Science Planning Team by ________________ [date], and thank you in advance for your kind consideration of this important matter.

Regards,

[signature and title]

Figure 7. Invitation to participate as a member of the SEM-Science planning team.

XX School
Schoolwide Enrichment Model-Science
Planning Team
Agenda

1. Welcome and Introductions
2. Purpose of the Schoolwide Enrichment Model in Science
3. Role of the Planning Team
4. People and Resources
5. Scheduling
6. Location
7. Reaching out

Figure 8. Example of agenda for first SEM-Science planning team meeting.

A SEM-Science Type I Documentation and Planning Form (Handout 12) has been provided to assist with the collection of this information during the meeting. Broadly speaking, the categories of Type I activities and resources that should be considered are: people, experiences in science, media, technology, and science materials. Each of these categories will be discussed further below, but for the purposes of the meeting, the goal is be to bring the team together to brainstorm and record ideas for each of six areas in science: biology, physics, chemistry, astronomy, Earth science, and engineering.

After the planning team's ideas are recorded, the topic of scheduling Type I science experiences and where to hold Type I science events should be addressed. Type I activities and events may be integrated into the science curriculum or they may be standalone events to which the entire school is invited. It really depends on the nature of the activity. For example, the entire school might be invited to hear a keynote speaker speak about her work on an archaeological dig in Egypt, whereas one class might be involved with a preliminary investigation on a topic. The team may wish to select a few overall Type I activities in which the whole school could participate and schedule, deciding on locations as appropriate. Team members will then need to concern themselves with how to organize and distribute the information on the remaining resources to the rest of the science faculty. For example, the information in Handout 12 could be placed on the school's website, along with an indication of when and where the event has been scheduled or where the resources are located to conduct the activity.

The SEM-Science planning team will be off to a good start, but it will be necessary to think about how to reach out to include other people. Most team members will have contacts and connections in the world of science and so the last activity may be to compile a list of these connections. Each team member could take a few to reach out to before the next meeting. For example, Team Member A might ask a doctor at the local hospital if he would be willing to speak at the school. Team Member B could check with the local science museum's curator, which might lead to a whole list of individuals. Thus at subsequent meetings of the SEM-Science planning team, the list of resources and activities in Handout 12 will continue to grow.

Type I Experiences

Type I science experiences are designed to promote students' enjoyment of and engagement in science. They are not meant to be comprehensive, or to teach everything there is about a topic. However, a few, not necessarily all, should trigger a desire in students to want to know more.

What are different types of Type I activities in science? For the purposes of this discussion, it may be helpful to think of them in terms of their focus—are they focused on people, experiences, media, or technology? We will call this the area of focus, and discuss each category in more depth.

Focus on People

Many engaging Type I activities in science will focus on people. In this area of focus, speakers are identified and brought into the classroom or school to discuss a wide range of topics or sometimes students will visit the speaker. These individuals might have an expertise in some area of science, or they might simply be individuals in the community working in an area related to science. Speakers in areas related to science might include:

- doctors and nurses,
- local science museum curators,
- zoologists,
- pet shop owners,
- rock collectors,
- geologists,
- scientists from a planetarium,
- faculty from a local university,
- veterinarians,
- local meteorologists,
- workers from a local plant nursery,
- pharmacists,
- physical therapists,
- manufacturers,
- computer technicians,
- authors of science books,
- nutritionists,
- mental health advocates,
- astronauts,
- engineers,
- architects,
- agriculturalists, and
- chemical processing plant workers.

Of course, this list is only a partial list of possible speakers. A good way to locate specific speakers near your school is through personal connections and also the connections of the planning team. However, the Internet is also a resource, allowing us to connect with one another far and wide. For example, the "Nifty Fifty" program in the Washington, DC area features 200 noted science and engineering professionals who will speak at middle and elementary schools (see http://www.usasciencefestival.org/schoolprograms/niftyfifty.html). New York City is fortunate enough to have a speakers' bureau for Earth scientists at (see http://earthdayny.org/speakers-bureau). If you live in another area, you might try searching for "elementary school science speakers near" and then insert the largest town or city near you.

Focus on Experiences

Experiences that occur inside or outside of the science classroom may also become the focus of a Type I activity. Science demonstrations, preliminary investigations, enrichment clusters, field trips, and interest development centers are all ideas for experience-oriented activities that may spark a desire in students to know more about a topic.

Science demonstrations. Used for decades in the classroom, science demonstrations usually consist of teachers showing students something that is engaging and designed in such a way as to introduce content knowledge to the class. The demonstration may also require materials that are too costly to allow students to do the activity themselves, or it may be too dangerous. For example, soaking a dollar bill in a solution of half alcohol and half water and then lighting it on fire will burn off the alcohol, but the water will protect the dollar bill. Students will see an impressive display of flames, but then the dollar bill will emerge, whole and unscathed. This useful demonstration may prove a useful way to "spark" students' interest in the properties of matter, but it is too unsafe to allow them to do on their own. Table 1 lists a few sites that may prove useful when getting started, but many more resources are available on the web.

Preliminary investigations. Sometimes a preliminary investigation into a science topic may trigger an ongoing interest and a desire to know more in a student. For example, examining a drop of pond water and seeing it teeming with microscopic life may be enough to initiate a lifelong interest in microbiology. Preliminary investigations, as we use them here, are meant to be quick, engaging, and the start to a longer unit of exploration.

Another type of preliminary investigation is the science fair. These traditional investigations take place over several weeks and may become the gateway

TABLE 1
WEBSITES WITH SCIENCE DEMONSTRATIONS

Provider— *Website Address* Description
ACS: Chemistry for Life— *http://www.acs.org/content/acs/en/education/resources/k-8/thebestof.html* ◆ A book, *Wonderscience*, that may be ordered, as well as free downloadable sample activities.
Elmhurst College— *http://www.elmhurst.edu/~chm/demos/demoh.html* ◆ Demonstrations on physical science.
Scholastic— *http://www.scholastic.com/teachers/article/40-cool-science-experiments-web* ◆ 40 science demonstrations viewed through YouTube.

to a deep, sustained interest in science or in a particular topic in science. For example, one of the authors knew a student who completed her science fair over several years on memory and the brain; today that student is a neuroscientist conducting research and teaching at a well-known university. Table 2 (Heilbronner, 2013b, p. 121) offers a number of websites containing interesting science investigations for children.

Enrichment clusters. Another way to engage science students is through enrichment clusters, which "focus students' attention on authentic learning applied to real-life problems" (National Research Center on the Gifted and Talented, n.d., part 1, para. 3). Much has been written about enrichment clusters, so many readers will be aware that they are interest-based groups that meet over the course of several weeks to work toward the production of a product or service. They are frequently led by a teacher, but they may also be led by someone outside the school with expertise in a particular topic. Additionally, clusters usually operate without lesson plans or curriculum. Frequently, multiple enrichment clusters are offered at one time, and students self-select a cluster based on their interest in a topic.

Many ideas for enrichment clusters in science come from children themselves, so it is frequently best to use the interest surveys from the SEM-Science Talent Portfolio to identify groups of interests. It is important to remember that some topics lend themselves to the development of enrichment clusters more than other topics. For example, an interest in dinosaurs may be more difficult to develop an enrichment cluster around than an interest in insects, because, unlike dinosaurs, insects are ubiquitous and present with us today.

A few examples of enrichment clusters in science have been provided in Table 3. More information about enrichment clusters is available on the National

TABLE 2
WEBSITES WITH SCIENCE INVESTIGATIONS FOR CHILDREN

Site— *Website Address* Description
Make Glowing Water— *http://www.youtube.com/watch?v=6hX8H66I62U* ◆ YouTube is filled with fun investigations such as this one and Flubber (see below).
Kids Science Experiments— *http://www.kids-science-experiments.com* ◆ This site includes many different science investigations, categorized by topic.
"Let's Investigate" by Ellen Booth Church (Published by Scholastic.com)— *http://www.scholastic.com/resources/article/lets-investigate* ◆ This is an online article about what's important to young children.
National Science Teachers' Association (NSTA)— *http://www.nsta.org* ◆ This site includes a wealth of resources for teachers and parents.
Science Kids, Science Experiments for Kids— *http://www.sciencekids.co.nz/experiments.html* ◆ Experiments, games, projects, lessons, quizzes, and more are provided on this site.
Fun Science Projects for Children: Ingredients for Flubber— *http://www.youtube.com/watch?v=NhmRKpCCQmE* ◆ This is just one fun science demonstration. To locate more video demonstrations on investigations, try typing in a search term (e.g., "balloons").
Steve Spangler Science— *http://www.stevespanglerscience.com* ◆ A wealth of science kits, projects, and toys.
SmarterEveryDay— *https://www.youtube.com/user/destinws2* ◆ This is a collection of science videos, where the creator tries to answer various science questions or myths, often with the help of his children or experts in various science fields.

TABLE 3
EXAMPLES OF ENRICHMENT CLUSTERS IN SCIENCE

Area of Science	Name	Authentic Problem
Biology	Save the Whales Society	Create a campaign to raise awareness about endangerment of whales due to over-hunting.
Physics	The Task Force	Develop an invention using the laws of physics that accomplishes a useful task.
Chemistry	Chemistry Detectives	Investigate the impact of harmful chemicals in our environment; organize and implement an action plan to have a positive impact.
Astronomy	The Star Gazers	Investigate anomalies in the universe and create a movie to be shown at the local planetarium.
Earth Science	Rock On Company	Investigate local geology and create a guide and toolkit for young rock collectors.
Engineering	The Robotics Engineering Company	Create a robot that accomplishes a task.

Research Center for the Gifted and Talented's website at http://www.gifted.uconn.edu/sem/semart01.html and also in *Enrichment Clusters: A Practical Plan for Real-World, Student-Driven Learning* (Renzulli, Gentry, & Reis, 2014).

Field trips. One of the most engaging Type I activities is the field trip, and in science the possibilities for field trips appear endless. Before discussing specific types of field trips, however, it's important to note that several questions must be asked and answered by those planning the outings:

- When will the trip take place?
- What is the cost of the trip? How should payment be made?
- What provisions will be made for students who can't afford the trip?
- What will the students be doing? How will the events of the trip "flow"?
- How many students will the site accommodate?
- What provisions for food are available on site?
- Will the students need to bring anything to the site?
- How will the trip reinforce students' classroom science learning or engage them in science?

(Adapted from Heilbronner, 2008)

When adults are asked what they remember about science class, they rarely respond that they remember the worksheets they completed or tests they took. They will frequently respond with either some memorable project they were able to do in class or with a field trip. Science may be woven into many different types of field trips, including the following:

- planetariums,
- zoos,
- hospitals,
- doctors' offices,
- airports,
- farms,
- laboratories,
- factories,
- science museums,
- natural museums,
- aquariums,
- botanical gardens,
- national or state parks,
- beaches, and
- ponds.

In addition to these field trips, many local areas will have specialized attractions that focus on science, such as NASA in Florida or Texas.

Focus on Materials

Frequently, students engage with science through hands-on materials; distinguished scientists, for example, have reported "mucking about" informally with materials from very young ages as a way to find out about the natural and man-made worlds (Feist, 2006; Sosniak, 1985; Subotnik & Steiner, 1993). Whether it's taking apart and putting together a computer or studying a drop of pond water under an inexpensive microscope, this curiosity for the world can be brought inside the classroom by simply bringing in the materials and making them available to students in the form of interest development centers.

Consisting of little more than a set of materials and perhaps some limited instructions, interest development centers can be mounted on a tri-fold board or simply placed on a table in the classroom. Time at the centers may be scheduled into an instructional period, or students may simply go to them for free-time exploration. These centers may be developed around a theme, or they may be stand-alone materials with which children may be encouraged to play. For example, centers developed around themes might include rocks, insects, microscopic algae, computers, stages of matter, chemical compounds, and more. These types of interest development centers frequently encourage students to explore the materials in a structured way, resulting in a more guided type of inquiry; for example, students might be given instructions about how to test the hardness of different types of rocks and materials.

Creating interest development centers using stand-alone materials is another way for teachers to encourage free exploration. Simply putting these materials on a table and allowing students to interact with them will support the type of free exploration and open inquiry that will inspire many children to want to know more about science. A list of these types of "muck-about" materials is provided in Table 4. Of course, some of the materials are more appropriate for older students, and no materials should be made available to students without an adult's supervision.

Focus on Media

In many cases, exposure to carefully selected media can be engaging for students. By media, we include:

- audio media—podcasts, songs, and more;

TABLE 4
INTEREST DEVELOPMENT CENTER MATERIALS

Science Strand	Materials	
Chemistry	• Beakers or other containers • Common chemical compounds and mixtures—baking soda, vinegar, salt, sugar, sand • Food substances (e.g., marshmallows)	• Food dye • Hot plate • Measuring cups • Medicine droppers • Tongs
Earth science	• Different types of rocks and minerals (e.g., metamorphic, sedimentary, igneous) • Rock collecting tools • Crystal grow kits	• Weather tools: thermometer, hydrometer, barometer, rainfall gauge, wind vane, anemometer, etc.
Life science	• Aquarium • Collecting materials • Fertilizer • Fish • Frogs • Herbs—dried and fresh • Lizards • Microscope	• Plants—flowering and vegetable • Potting soil • Salamanders • Seeds • Turtles • Yeast • Worms
Physical science	• Balloons • Bouncing balls of different sizes and types • Metronome • Mirrors • Old electronic equipment (e.g., radio, phone, television, fans, computers, etc.)	• Pliers • Pulleys • Rope • Rubber bands • Scissors • Tuning fork • Wire
General	• Anti-bacterial cleanser • Baby food jars (emptied) • Balances • Batteries • Building sets (e.g., Kinex and LEGOs) • Buttons • Clay or playdough • Construction paper • Cooking oil • Flashlights • Foam peanuts • Gloves (latex free) • Glue • Hammer and nails • Paper cups	• Pipe cleaners • Plastic spoons • Rulers • Sandpaper • Saw • Screwdriver • Shoe boxes • Soda straws • Sponges • Steel wool • String • Tape • Toothpicks • Wax • Wax paper • Wood pieces

Note. Reprinted from "Raising Future Scientists" (p. 118) by N. Heilbronner, 2013, *Gifted Child Today, 36*(2). Copyright 2013 by SAGE Publications. Reprinted with permission.

- visual media—television, movies, and video;
- books; and
- newspapers and magazines.

Audio and visual media. A sample listing of audio and visual media appropriate to a classroom is provided in Table 5.

It is interesting to note the addition of "science fiction" pieces such as *The Twilight Zone* to the inventory. Do not discount the power of science fiction, for established scientists credit the genre for turning them on to science in general, and a number of inventions have been inspired from science fiction (Sydell, 2010).

Books. Books come in print and electronic forms, and a number of excellent bibliographies exist online. A few good sites that review books are mentioned in Table 6.

Newspapers and magazines. Through the years, teachers have subscribed to children's newspapers and magazines and saved articles that relate to students' learning. Today is no different, but teachers today have access to a wide variety of these types of media in science, as well as new ways to collect them for future use. For example, organizers such as Pinterest (http://www.pinterest.com) allow educators to peruse the Internet for interesting websites and then "pin" them to a virtual bulletin board. Another, Pocket, allows the user to store the website for later offline reading. Articles from children's newspapers and magazines may thus be marked, clipped, and saved for later use. A sample of children's magazines are included in Table 7.

Focus on Technology

Technology in the form of computer websites and apps can be a powerful motivator to learn more in science. Many websites and apps contain investigations that students will want to try, demonstrations that teachers can use, or simply a wealth of science information that is frequently accompanied by beautiful and inspiring photography. Examples of some of these types of websites are in Table 8.

Other types of technology include probes, apps, clickers, and more. These types of technology are covered in more depth in Chapter 8.

TABLE 5
SAMPLE AUDIO AND VISUAL CLASSROOM MEDIA IN SCIENCE

Title of Channel of Program—*Website or Fan Site Address* Description
Songs
Science Songs and Videos—*http://www.learninggamesforkids.com/science_songs.html*
Songs for Teaching—*http://www.songsforteaching.com/index.html* ◆ Contains many different science songs and their lyrics, as well as other products.
The Totally Free Children's Learning Network—*http://www.kidsknowit.com/educational-songs/index.php* ◆ Contains many science songs categorized by topic area.
Television
Animal Planet—*http://animal.discovery.com* ◆ Offers many shows on animals of all kinds. The website also offers video clips and games.
Discovery Channel—*http://dsc.discovery.com* ◆ Offers a number of high-quality science shows, including *Dinosaur Revolution*, *Mythbusters*, *Shark Week*, and more.
Dragonfly TV—*http://pbskids.org/dragonflytv*
Science Fiction—Television and Movies
Contact ◆ Starring Jody Foster, this film imagines what it might be like if Earth were contacted by extra-terrestrial beings.
Quantum Leap—*http://www.projectquantumleap.com* ◆ Documents the travels of a scientist as he leaps through time in an effort to right wrongs.
Star Trek Series—*http://www.startrek.com* ◆ Offers several highly engaging science fiction series, all set in a common "Star Trek" universe.
The Twilight Zone—*http://www.twilightzone.org* ◆ Decades ago, Rod Serling hosted this popular show using a science fiction format. You may wish to screen content for level of intensity.
Video
Bill Nye the Science Guy—*http://www.billnye.com* ◆ Highly engaging science video clips (under "Media"). Full videos may be purchased.
Brainpop—*http://www.brainpop.com* ◆ Engaging animated science videos. Also contains quizzes, experiments, and more.
National Geographic—*http://kids.nationalgeographic.com* ◆ Long known for high quality work in the natural world, these videos and games are geared toward children.

Note. Adapted from "Raising Future Scientists" (p. 119) by N. Heilbronner, 2013, *Gifted Child Today*, 36(2). Copyright 2013 by SAGE Publications. Adapted with permission.

TABLE 6
WEBSITES CONTAINING BIBLIOGRAPHIES
OF SCIENCE BOOKS FOR CHILDREN

Title of Website—*Website Address* Description
Kids' Nonfiction— *http://www.mariannedyson.com/spacebooks.htm* ◆ Books on space are reviewed by author and NASA flight controller Marianne Dyson.
Popular Science Books for Children— *http://www.popularscience.co.uk/books%20children.htm* ◆ Summaries and reviews are provided.
Science Books for Kids— *http://www.science-books-for-kids.com* ◆ Best of 2011—books are divided into categories by topics and age.
Surprising Science: Great Science Books for the Little Ones— *http://blogs.smithsonianmag.com/science/2010/12/great-science-books-for-the-little-ones* ◆ Published by the Smithsonian, this list contains reviews of high-quality books.

Note. Adapted from "Raising Future Scientists" (p. 119) by N. Heilbronner, 2013, *Gifted Child Today*, 36(2). Copyright 2013 by SAGE Publications. Adapted with permission.

TABLE 7
CHILDREN'S MAGAZINES THAT FOCUS ON SCIENCE

Title	Description
Ask	Good for ages 7–10, each issue focuses on arts and sciences.
Chickadee	Packed with science games, experiments, and photos for children ages 6–9.
Click	Covers science, nature, and the environment for children ages 3–7.
Muse	Sponsored by the Smithsonian, *Muse* is appropriate for ages 9–14.
Odyssey	Covers the hottest trends in science for ages 10 and above.
Ranger Rick	For ages 7 and up, Ranger Rick is the oldest children's magazine in print.
Zoobooks	Great for students ages 6–12 who love animals, each issue has a group of animals as its theme.

After the Type I Activity

As with Type I activities in other subject areas, it's important to follow the activity with some type of debriefing experience. The idea here is to "stimulate new interests that might lead to follow-up by students who share a common interest" (Renzulli & Reis, 2014, p. 119). Speakers might be invited to stay and meet with students who want to plan additional study and possibly a Type III project. Teachers might lead a classroom discussion that also functions as a debriefing, focusing on what students liked and were interested in, whether

TABLE 8
ENGAGING WEBSITES FOR SCIENCE CLASS

Title of Website—*Website Address* **Description**
Astronomy
Eyes on the Solar System— *http://eyes.nasa.gov/download.html* • Students direct a NASA mission; requires a one-time download.
NASA Kids Club—*http://www.nasa.gov/audience/forkids/kidsclub/flash/index.html* • Students learn about space at this site.
Earth Science
Climate Kids— *http://climatekids.nasa.gov* • Produced by NASA, the site introduces children to the topic of climate change.
Earth Rangers— *http://www.earthrangers.com* • A beautiful website containing activities and information about protecting the Earth and animals.
Farmers' Almanac— *http://www.almanac4kids.com* • Contains a student version of the old-time favorite.
Engineering
Engineer Girl— *http://www.engineergirl.org* • A service of the National Academy of Engineering, the site contains information designed to interest girls in engineering and provide them with resources to become engineers.
Life Science
Arkive—*http://www.arkive.org* • Contains information and stunning photos of the world's endangered species.
Frontiers for Young Minds— *http://kids.frontiersin.org* • Students can serve as authors, mentors, or editors in this creative kids' journal on neuroscience.
Physical Science/Engineering
Bob the Builder—*http://www.bobthebuilder.com/usa/index.asp* • Contains activities, projects, games, and more that teach about physical science and construction.
ChemiCool— *http://www.chemicool.com* • Provides an interactive chart of chemical elements; when students click on an element, they are taken to a page describing the history, uses, and much more about the element.
Quarked!— *http://www.quarked.org* • Allows students to explore the world of particle physics.
Science—General
Discovery Kids— *http://discoverykids.com* • Contains many games, activities, and much information, all attractively packaged, for students on a variety of topics.
National Geographic for Kids— *http://kids.nationalgeographic.com* • Great resource for learning about the world, its people, and its wildlife.
Internet4Classrooms: Science Resources— *http://www.internet4classrooms.com/science.htm* • An excellent resource for science teachers that also contains a number of virtual activities for students.
Ology— *http://www.amnh.org/explore/ology* • Sponsored by the Smithsonian Institute, the website encourages exploration of a wide variety of science content.

they'd like to pursue the topic further, and what projects come to mind regarding the topic.

Students may also be encouraged individually to explore their topics of interest by exposing them to Type I experiences. Students may communicate their interest in a scientific topic through the Science Style Action Information Form (Handout 13). For example, suppose a teacher invites an engineer to speak to the class, and he discusses his work on the International Space Station. One of the students, Jaime, appears incredibly excited by everything the engineer has to say. He asks extensive questions and even wants to have his picture taken with the engineer. He asks the engineer how he knew he wanted to become an engineer. After, he completes a Science Style Information Action Information Form (Handout 13) and gives it to his teacher, who will begin to consider how to guide him to complete a Type III investigation using methods discussed in later chapters.

Evaluation of Type I activities is also a component of SEM-Science, for a number of reasons. First, it enables the SEM-Science planning team to understand which activities were effective at inspiring students to explore a topic further, such as through the completion of Type III projects. Second, evaluation can also provide documentation regarding how valuable students and teachers believed the experience to be. Third, evaluation can provide documentation in a growing era of school-based accountability that the experience was worthwhile. Evaluation can thus become an ongoing component of the Type I planning team's agenda and provide valuable information regarding whether the activity should take place again in the future. Evaluation forms for general Type I activities that may be applied to science may be found in the third edition of *The Schoolwide Enrichment Model* (Renzulli & Reis, 2014, pp. 121–125).

HANDOUT 12

Schoolwide Enrichment Model in Science Type I Documentation and Planning Form

Grade level(s): ____________________

	Biology	Physics	Chemistry	Astronomy	Earth Science	Engineering
People						
Speakers in Science						
Science Mentors						
Science Coaches						
Other						
Experiences						
Demonstrations						
Preliminary Investigations						
Enrichment Clusters						
Field Trips						
Interest Development Centers						
Other						
Science Media						
Film						
Television Programs/ DVDs						
Newspaper or Magazines						
Books						
Technology						
Websites						
Virtual Field Trips						
Simulations						
Other Websites						
Apps						
Videos						
Materials						
Lab Materials						
Cooking/Kitchen						
Construction						
Instruments						

Name: Date:

HANDOUT 12, CONTINUED

	Biology	**Physics**	**Chemistry**	**Astronomy**	**Earth Science**	**Engineering**
Animal Care						
Animals						
Household Appliances						
Musical						
Gardening						
Cleaning						
Containers						

Name: Date:

HANDOUT 13

Science Style—Action Information Form

Directions: Fill out this form and hand it to your teacher if you are interested in learning more about a science topic.

1. What is the topic that you would like to study?

2. What interests you about this topic?

3. When did your interest in this topic begin?

4. How did your interest in this topic begin?

CHAPTER 5

Developing Type II Skills in Science

After engaging students with science content through Type I activities, they must be taught to work the way that actual scientists work. Students may be taught to think and act like junior practitioners by encouraging them to "do" science through Type II skills. In SEM-Science, the objective of teaching students Type II skills is to give them the tools necessary to produce a Type III project, but in reality, teaching students Type II skills will also empower them to begin to think and act like practitioners as they set about implementing science practices that will enable them to accomplish authentic work.

Type II Skills in Science

What are Type II skills in science? If we consider the type of work that practicing scientists do, it's easy to understand that students must learn certain science skills if they are to engage in authentic work.

In his noted book, *Outliers: The Story of Success* (2007), author Malcolm Gladwell claimed that it takes an individual roughly 10,000 hours of practice to become an expert in a field, and scientists are no exception. Every day as scientists go about their jobs, they each carry with them an intellectual and emotional "toolkit" of skills that have been carefully honed over time—this toolkit is essential for them to perform the work in their fields. They didn't always have the toolkit, and the important thing to realize is that *they had to start somewhere.* Our students are starting to build their toolkits, and we can be the ones who help them get off to a good start. However, what goes in the toolkit? In other words, what are the Type II skills that students in science could be taught? Again, by considering how scientists work, it's easier to understand what goes in the toolkit.

Many people believe that scientists use the scientific method every day to conduct investigations on topics of interest. However, in reality, scientists use the inquiry method, which is:

> a multifaceted activity that involves making observations; posing questions; examining books and other sources of information to see what is already known; planning investigations; reviewing what is already known in light of experimental evidence; using tools to gather, analyze, and interpret data; proposing answers, explanations, and predictions; and communicating the results. (National Academies Press, 1996, p. 23)

Two primary differences between the five- or six-step scientific method taught in many classrooms and the process of inquiry are that inquiry is more reflective and iterative in nature, and the scientific method focuses almost exclusively on conducting experiments, while inquiry broadens that focus to include other types of investigations such as observations. The teaching of inquiry in the science classroom encourages students to become reflective critical thinkers and is encouraged by The National Research Council, the National Science Teachers' Association, and the National Academies of Science.

Scientists and science educators have identified the skills or "practices" required to carry out inquiry in the classroom. These practices are classified into two levels—basic and integrated. Basic science process skills or practices are simpler and provide a foundation for learning (Lancour, 2008; Padilla, 1990). They include observing, inferring, measuring, communicating, classifying, and predicting. Integrated practices are more advanced and allow students to conduct investigations into topics. Concurrent with a renewed interest in developing engineers, the National Research Council (NRC, 2012) has defined a list of practices that includes sometimes separate skills for engineers, whose focus is more on defining problems and designing solutions to those problems. The NRC defined the scientific and engineering practices as:

1. Asking questions (for science) and defining problems (for engineering).
2. Developing and using models.
3. Planning and carrying out investigations.

4. Analyzing and interpreting data.
5. Using mathematics and computational thinking.
6. Constructing explanations (for science) and designing solutions (for engineering).
7. Engaging in argument from evidence.
8. Obtaining, evaluating, and communicating information. (p. 42)

These are also the skills that are identified in the current Next Generation Science Standards as science and engineering practices (Leo, Quinn, & Valdes, 2013).

Although these skills are important to inquiry, students must acquire other skills before they can think and act like scientists. Four strands of proficiency (Michaels et al., 2008) organize the NGSS and the additional skills into interwoven threads that offer a new and productive way to think about how to teach science. The purpose of Type II skills is to provide a link between Type I activities that engage and interest students and Type III activities, in which students are able to extend and apply knowledge to create a project that is meaningful and authentic. Type II skills therefore enable students to understand content, generate scientific evidence, reflect on their own knowledge, and participate productively in science. These strands and the categories of Type II skills that are most closely aligned with each skill in science are presented in Table 9, along with specific examples of each skill. You will note that NGSS practices are distributed throughout several of these strands.

Each of these categories is discussed in more depth below.

Learning and Research

Learning and research occurs in children from a very young age as they open their eyes to the world around them, and learning science content allows them to understand and explain this world. Listening and observing are two of the most basic ways that children begin to understand their environment. For example, a child might be walking beside a meadow in the spring and observe a chrysalis attached to a small branch. If she travels along the same route each day, she might notice the chrysalis is dormant until one day, a butterfly emerges. She might also hear a bird call and want to know more about what she witnesses and so she may read about the birds and butterflies on the Internet. Or she might go to her school's library and peruse the many books there on these animals. In this case, she is constructing knowledge based on the skills of observation and research; she is also using technology to assist her in doing her research.

TABLE 9
SCIENCE STRANDS OF PROFICIENCY AND THEIR ALIGNED TYPE II SKILLS

Strand	Description	Category	Example of Type II Skills
1. Understanding Scientific Explanations	Students learn scientific content so that they may apply it to the natural world to explain phenomena	Learning and research	Listening Observing Sketching Photographing Reading Reference skills Technology skills Note-taking Outlining
2. Generating Scientific Evidence	Students build and refine models, design and analyze investigations, and construct and defend arguments with evidence	Scientific practices—NGSS (2013) Creativity Critical thinking	Scientific practices • Asking questions • Developing solutions • Developing and using models • Planning and carrying out investigations • Analyzing and interpreting data • Using mathematics and computational thinking • Constructing explanations • Engaging in argument from evidence Creativity Creative problem solving Critical and logical thinking skills
3. Reflecting on Scientific Knowledge	Students think about their own learning and build upon it	Reflective practices	Evaluating information Evaluating methods Evaluating risks Evaluating motives Tolerance for the unknown
4. Participating Productively in Science	Students communicate and collaborate with others to advance the body of scientific knowledge; students understand the ways that scientists are expected to behave	Communication practices Affective training	Communicating information: • Written communication • Oral communication • Technological communication Collaboration

The example above focuses on students' learning in informal settings, but of course much learning also takes place in more formal settings such as the classroom. Students learn to listen to and observe the world around them, a not inconsequential skill that must be honed over time. Even very young children can be taught to focus on their environment to become more aware of its wonders. Sketching or photographing what is in that world may help—practicing scientists use these skills each day to record their observations and changes that happen over time. Students may be encouraged to keep a journal with these observations and sketches.

A skill with which students sometimes struggle is reading nonfiction, and graphic organizers can be most helpful in aiding students to organize and understand the information. Trips to the school's library may expand their content knowledge, but students still need to understand how to use media skills to locate information. Technology has exploded exponentially over the last few decades, and todays' students have information at their fingertips—sometimes too much information. They require the ability to use advanced reference skills to locate information and then to sort through this vast sea of information to evaluate what is relevant, trustworthy, and useful to their purpose. Finally, students may need assistance such as note-taking or outlining skills to help them to organize the content they are learning.

Scientific Practices

In addition to learning content in the manner described above, students of science must learn practices of the discipline that enable them to generate evidence to support their ideas. These scientific practices are not unique to science, but they are tools frequently used by scientists. For example, scientists might build or analyze a model to understand large-scale systems or design an experiment to investigate hypotheses and then gather the results of these investigations to generate evidence for their ideas. In the same manner, students may be taught to think and act like junior scientists. It is true that they will probably not generate new and groundbreaking research, but the important thing to understand is that *it will be new and groundbreaking to them.*

Scientific practices allow us to understand and solve problems and to construct and evaluate evidence to do so. These scientific practices include (NRC, 2012):

› asking questions (for science) and defining problems (for engineering),
› developing and using models,
› planning and carrying out investigations,

- analyzing and interpreting data,
- using mathematic and computational thinking,
- constructing explanations (for science) and designing solutions (for engineering), and
- engaging in argument from evidence.

It is important to note the role of three additional skills in the interplay of these practices: creativity, creative problem solving, and critical and logical thinking skills. Creativity and creative problem solving skills are related halves of the same whole, and it may be surprising to think about how much engineers and sciences use and apply these skills. Researchers (Sternberg, Kaufman, & Pretz, 2002) have defined creativity as "the ability to produce work that is novel (i.e., original, unexpected), high in quality, and appropriate (i.e., useful, meets task constraints)." Noted researcher E. Paul Torrance suggested that there were four types of creativity: fluency, flexibility, originality, and elaboration. Fluency has to do with coming up with many ideas—an engineer who can think of many different uses for a material, for example, is said to be fluent in this area. Flexibility is more about putting a new twist on an old idea. For example, the engineers who combined computer technology with motion sensors have been able to produce some fairly realistic and engaging simulated video worlds through gaming. Originality means generating new ideas, as Charles Darwin did when he developed his ideas about natural selection, and elaboration means extending ideas, such as when inventor Dean Kamen miniaturized the dialysis machine to make it portable.

Creative problem solving is a specific method used by practitioners in many fields to develop solutions to various problems by applying creative methods. As originally proposed by advertising tycoon Alex Osborne, the method consists of five linear steps: investigate the problem; identify the actual problem; generate ideas about how to solve the problem; evaluate those ideas to select a solution; and generate acceptance about the solution. Countless inventions have been developed this way—think, for example, of the incorporation of the camera into smartphone technology. The actual problem with cameras was not that we needed more types or better cameras—digital technology had evolved to the point that cameras were tiny and performed effectively. The real problem was that most of us didn't want to carry two devices at once—a phone and a camera; it required the genius of Steve Jobs and Apple to understand the nature and the opportunities presented by the real problem, and the solution that was generated was the first iPhone with an embedded camera. Students can be taught these steps and learn how to apply them to problems inside and outside the science classroom.

If creativity is the generation of many or original ideas, critical and logical thinking skills allow students to hone in and evaluate ideas. Thought of in this way, creativity is focused outward on the development of many ideas, while critical and logical thinking skills are focused inward, enabling students to narrow and select the best ideas. Critical thinking skills empower us to evaluate evidence and make decisions, and in science they allow us to analyze data for patterns in order to make conclusions. Also, in this day and age of information overload, developing students' ability to evaluate that information whatever the source (books, Internet, friends) has become especially important and relevant.

Reflective Practices

Scientists, like teachers, must take time to evaluate the way that they are doing things. In teachers, reflection frequently involves thinking about how a lesson went, how the strategies that were used may have impacted the learn outcomes, and how to manipulate the lesson to improve the outcomes. In science, reflection usually means thinking about how an investigation or experiment went, how the methodologies that were used may have impacted the results, and how to change the investigation to build upon the outcomes. A scientist might decide that a particular approach did not work well because it was not able to yield the types of data he or she needed to investigate a phenomenon. For example, in the 1940s, Rosalind Franklin worked to understand the structure of DNA. She collaborated with a partner, Maurice Wilkins, and together they tried to understand DNA's structure by using a then-new technology called x-ray diffraction. James Watson and Francis Crick were also working together at the same time on the same problem, only they were developing DNA models. Neither group knew everything they needed to know to solve the problem; it was only when Franklin realigned herself with Watson and Crick and they combined the two methods that they were able to understand the true nature of DNA.

Similarly, students can be taught to be reflective of their own methodologies and relate them to outcomes. For example, when conducting a science investigation on density, students might be taught that weight (mass) is one variable that affects whether an object sinks or floats. They might then be given two objects that weigh the same—for example, a paper clip and a wood cork. They drop them in water and deduce that another variable must be at work, because even though the items weigh the same, the paper clip sinks and the cork floats. They might then be encouraged by their teacher to revise their methods to determine how to test other factors and therefore deduce what the additional variable might be (it is volume).

In addition to reflection of methodologies, scientists must regularly reflect upon and evaluate the risks involved with their investigations. This is an important consideration, especially in light of some dangerous new technologies that have been developed over the 20th century. For example, physicists working on the Hadron Collider had to ask themselves continually about the risk involved with creating super-fast particles, which have a very tiny chance of creating a miniature black hole. On the one hand, they had to realistically assess the risk (tiny) and also weigh their own desires for achievement and fame; on the other hand, they had to assess the potential for benefits that could arise from discoveries made using the collider. In the end, they made the choice that the benefits far outweighed the risks, and so the collider operates today. Of course, students aren't designing Hadron Colliders, but they could be placing living beings at risk with simple experiments. For example, a student who wants to do an investigation involving animals must be taught that certain types of experiments (e.g., ones that cause pain in the animal) are off-limits.

Another consideration involves teaching students to honestly assess their own motives, especially in terms of how they conduct their investigations. More than one scientist has fallen prey to slanting the results of his or her investigations to suit his or her own biases. Although this tendency is the result of human nature, it is one that we must monitor, because science itself is built on the integrity of its practitioners and on the honest assessment of outcomes. In an even worse situation, a few scientists have also been known to falsify data in order to obtain the outcomes they desire. Of course, this practice is unethical, and students must be taught that one of the safeguards built into science is the idea that studies must be replicable. If they are replicable, other scientists should be able to obtain similar results; if they do not, something must explain the differences in findings. A few possibilities include the fact that the original study was flawed, that the two studies were not identical, or that the data were falsified.

In addition to these reflective skills, students must develop an affect for science, and this usually includes a healthy tolerance for the unknown. Scientists work with a number of unknowns, especially while conducting investigations. It is not always easy or clear to understand just how to develop an investigation, or what the outcomes will be, and sometimes a final answer eludes us because of the nature of the investigation. Consider, for example, the nature of the universe—scientists concede that distance and time make the universe difficult to study, and some things may never be known. In class, students may be taught a tolerance for the unknown.

Participating Productively in Science

Sir Isaac Newton once famously said, "If I have seen further, it is only by standing on the shoulders of giants." Scientists collaborate and communicate with each other in order to share their discoveries and build upon them. This communication might take the form of written communication, oral communication, or technological communication. For example, scientists write papers to publish in scientific journals, they present orally at conferences, as well as in more informal settings, and they use technology to present their ideas through PowerPoint presentations and more.

Students may not be presenting their ideas at international conferences, but they can be taught to use the power of written and oral language, as well as technology, to distribute their ideas to a wider audience beyond the classroom. For example, the *Journal of Emerging Investigators* (http://www.emerginginvestigators.org) publishes research by middle and high school students. Or teachers may start their own journals to publish articles written by students and even include a peer-review step in the process. Students may use technology to develop presentations regarding their work and then give a talk to relevant community groups such as school boards, county commissions, and more.

A final Type II skill that is invaluable to scientists and that students will need to develop is collaboration, or the ability to work productively with one another. Scientists rarely work in a vacuum—they build their discoveries collaboratively with other scientists, and so good communication patterns and respect for each other is necessary. Similarly, group work in the classroom can be encouraged at times to ensure that students build this necessary skill.

Developing Type II Skills in Students

Teachers of enrichment programs, as well as teachers of regular classrooms, will want to develop these skills throughout the academic year. To do so, careful planning is necessary, and so a Materials and Activities Selection Worksheet for Planning Type II Enrichment in Science is provided in Handout 14. The sheet is versatile, and so the SEM-Science committee might use it to plan curricular activities and resources for the school or grade for an entire academic year, or a single teacher might use it to plan for his or her own class of students.

Teachers will want to develop Type II skills in each of these areas as they progress through the curriculum in science, but the learning should be targeted toward the eventual implementation of an authentic learning project, a Type III activity. That is, the ultimate goal of teaching students how to use a secchi disk might be so that they can measure the turbidity of the local river and relate those findings in a Type III project designed to make citizens aware of local pollutants and their effects on the river. However, until students arrive at the point where they can apply these skills to an authentic learning performance, there are several levels of learning:

› basic knowledge,
› "dress-rehearsal," and
› authentic performance.

Basic Knowledge—Learning the Skill

In the basic knowledge stage, the student learns about the skill—what it is, how it may be used, and when it is appropriate to do so. For example, a student might learn that an interview consists of seeking out someone with special knowledge or background relevant to the topic, developing questions to ask that person, meeting with him or her to ask the questions, and recording the answers. The student would also want to know the less obvious aspects of the skill, such as how to ask the questions, the ethics of revealing the purpose of the interview and gaining the participant's permission, and more.

Dress Rehearsal—Practicing the Skill

Like a dress rehearsal during a play, this stage gives students the opportunity to try out the skill before "performing" it, usually with other students in the classroom or with a friend or family member. Role-playing may therefore be involved. For example, if the Type II skill is interviewing, the student might interview a classmate regarding a topic—either a topic provided by the teacher, a topic of interest to the student, or a topic that will eventually become the student's Type III activity. Feedback on the skill is essential at this point as the student strives to improve, and several cycles of practice may be necessary.

Authentic Performance—Applying the Skill

Now the student understands the skill and has had practice applying it. He or she is ready for the "authentic performance," which can be thought of as the opening night of a play, a time in which the skill is applied for the purpose of developing authentic work. Perhaps the student will interview experts on pollution to understand the sources of pollution in the river, or perhaps the work will be focused on interviewing members of a local council to understand the rules and regulations regarding safeguarding the environment. Both of these interviews might allow the student to implement a Type III project designed to clean up the local river.

As teachers, we need to provide our students with a classroom learning environment where they can learn the skill, practice it, and then apply it to a real-life situation. A Type II Skills Monitoring Sheet for individual students is provided in Handout 15. Using this sheet will ensure that each student is receiving the type of practice that he or she needs before moving on to authentic application of the skills. A Classroom Monitoring Sheet, provided in Handout 16, enables the teacher to ensure that the entire class is exposed to each of the skills at some point.

HANDOUT 14

Materials and Activities Selection Worksheet for Planning Type II Enrichment in Science

Teacher(s): ____

____ Grade: ______________

		Regular Classroom	
	Enrichment Program	Group Activities	Self-Selected Activities
1. Understanding Scientific Explanations			
a. Listening			
b. Observing			
c. Sketching			
d. Photographing			
e. Reading			
f. Reference Skills			
g. Technology Skills			
h. Note-Taking/Outlining			
2. Generating Scientific Evidence			
a. Science Practices			
b. Creativity Skills			
c. Creative Problem Solving Skills			
d. Critical and Logical Thinking Skills			
3. Reflecting on Scientific Knowledge			
a. Evaluating Methods			
b. Evaluating Risks			
c. Evaluating Motives			
d. Tolerance for the Unknown			
4. Participating Productively in Science			
a. Written Communication			
b. Oral Communication			
c. Technological Communication			
d. Collaboration			

HANDOUT 15

Type II Enrichment—Student Monitoring (Individual)

Teacher(s): ______________________________

______________________________ Grade: ______________

Student Name	Type II Skill	Level Mastered: Basic Knowledge	Level Mastered: Dress Rehearsal	Level Mastered: Authentic Performance	Notes
	Understanding Scientific Explanations				
	Listening				
	Observing				
	Sketching				
	Photographing				
	Reading Nonfiction				
	Reference Skills				
	Technology Skills				
	Note-Taking				
	Outlining				
	Interviewing				
	Surveying				
	Generating Scientific Evidence				
	Creativity Skills				

HANDOUT 15, CONTINUED

Student Name	Type II Skill	Level Mastered: Basic Knowledge	Level Mastered: Dress Rehearsal	Level Mastered: Authentic Performance	Notes
	Creative Problem Solving Skills				
	Critical and Logical Thinking Skills				
	Basic Science Process Skills				
	Science Practices				
	Reflecting on Science Knowledge				
	Evaluating Methods				
	Evaluating Risks				
	Evaluating Motives				
	Tolerance for the Unknown				
	Participating Productively in Science				
	Written Communication				
	Oral Communication				
	Technological Communication				
	Collaboration				

HANDOUT 16

Type II Enrichment—Classroom

Teacher(s): ______________________________

______________________________ Grade: ______________

Type II Skill	Level Mastered: Basic Knowledge	Level Mastered: Dress Rehearsal	Level Mastered: Authentic Performance	Notes
Understanding Scientific Explanations				
Listening				
Observing				
Sketching				
Photographing				
Reading Nonfiction				
Reference Skills				
Technology Skills				
Note-Taking				
Outlining				
Interviewing				
Surveying				
Generating Scientific Evidence				
Creativity Skills				

HANDOUT 16, CONTINUED

Type II Skill	Level Mastered: Basic Knowledge	Level Mastered: Dress Rehearsal	Level Mastered: Authentic Performance	Notes
Creative Problem Solving Skills				
Critical and Logical Thinking Skills				
Basic Science Process Skills				
Science Practices				
Reflecting on Science Knowledge				
Evaluating Methods				
Evaluating Risks				
Evaluating Motives				
Tolerance for the Unknown				
Participating Productively in Science				
Written Communication				
Oral Communication				
Technological Communication				
Collaboration				

CHAPTER 6

Type III Activities—Developing Meaningful Investigations in Science

It is well-known in education that students learn best when engaged in a purposeful and meaningful activity. This can happen within the science classroom, but when the activity has application beyond the walls of the classroom, students intuitively sense the importance of what they are doing and engagement increases dramatically. In the SEM, one of the ultimate goals is to prepare advanced students to complete Type III activities—they have been working toward this goal all along. Type I activities lay the groundwork, providing students with a multitude of interests to explore. Type II activities in science provide students with the toolkit of skills they need to complete their work, and Type III activities provide the meaning and purpose by allowing students to apply those skills to complete an authentic project.

Because of its investigative nature, science as a domain lends itself to the development of authentic Type III activities. But what is a Type III activity in science? What does it look and feel like? As in the regular SEM, Type III activities in science are defined by a certain number of characteristics (see Table 10). The first defining characteristic of a Type III activity in science is that the learner assumes control of the learning, so science knowledge and skills are applied to produce an authentic project in science. Students also select the form that their projects will take—the work that they will produce. Therefore, the student takes on the role of junior practitioner, the scientist in the laboratory or field, and the teacher becomes the facilitator—the "guide on the side" who provides logistical help and oversight of the project. Teachers might do a variety of tasks to assist students throughout the Type III activity, including helping them to organize

TABLE 10
DEFINING CHARACTERISTICS OF THE TYPE III ACTIVITY IN SCIENCE

Definition	Investigative activity in which the learner assumes control of the learning; science knowledge and skills are applied to produce an authentic project in science. The learner takes on the role of a practicing scientist.
Objectives	1. To increase students' science content knowledge as they explore the topic at an advanced level. 2. To provide students with opportunities to apply and practice Type II science skills. 3. To provide students with organizational and logistical skills that they may apply in other everyday situations. 4. To develop task-commitment and confidence as they complete meaningful work and see the fruits of that work.
Notification	Science Style—Action Information Form.
Target Audience	Individuals or small groups of students who demonstrate sincere interests in science topics and who show a willingness to pursue these topics at advanced levels of involvement.
Origin	Topic should be of interest to the student.
Product	Product should be selected by the student, with the guidance of the teacher. Project should have application beyond the walls of the classroom.

their projects, to make wise choices, to communicate to others, and to procure resources.

With this type of arrangement, many purposes are served. First, the student is encouraged to learn about a topic more deeply than ever before. By completing more advanced projects, students will need to research topics in books, magazines, Internet and journal articles, videos, and more. Next, students will utilize the "tools" in their science "toolkit" to build something of significance. Type II science skills—learning and research skills, science practices, reflective practices, and more—will be applied as students drive toward the completion of their projects. Also, in the process, students will acquire logistical and organizational skills related to project management, such as budgeting and time management. Finally, students will develop task-commitment, or the ability to apply themselves over increasingly longer periods to complete their goals, as well as the confidence necessary to undertake these types of activities.

Students generally notify their teacher that they wish to do an individual Type III activity after some type of initial exploration of a topic—generally a Type I exploration. However, because of their investigative nature, Type III activities in science lend themselves to group exploration that may be woven into the everyday curriculum in a classroom.

Type III projects are generally developed for an authentic audience—that is, the audience has a sincere interest in the topic and is usually located outside of the classroom. In science, the audience for a Type III project might be the curators for a local science museum, the members of the university's biology department, or the residents of a nursing home, depending on the topic. The audience's interest in the topic should be genuine, and they may wish to advance the work of the student's Type III investigation in some way. For example, students who complete a project on mapping the local plant life in a nearby forest might present their project to the university's biology department, who might then analyze the information to understand patterns of flora in relationship to a number of factors such as sunlight, rainfall, and pollution.

Type III activities should challenge all students, and the time and effort that must be expended by all students should be roughly the same. Frequently, talented students put forth little effort on regular learning in the classroom, and so they never internalize the amount of work required to strive for excellence. Because of the nature of Type III activities, they are interesting to students and will engage and motivate them as they learn to apply sustained effort toward self-directed learning, so the task should not be something that can be accomplished easily. It must be doable, yet require effort.

The essential elements of a Type III investigation therefore include the following:

1. personalization of interest—the student(s) selects the topic;
2. use of authentic methodology—involves some kind of original data gathering or creative expression;
3. no existing solution or "right" answer; and
4. designed to have an impact on an audience other than or in addition to the teacher.

What might a Type III activity look like in science? By exploring two examples, it is possible to gain an understanding of how these activities fit into the classroom. Although these examples are fictitious, they are drawn from countless real-life stories of students who completed Type III activities. In the first example, Dan is a fourth-grade student with a keen interest in learning about medicine and the body, and in the final example, Carla is a 10th-grade student who enjoys mathematics and its applications to science.

For as long as he could remember, Dan had wanted to become some type of physician. His teacher, Mrs. S., saw the interest immediately after the school year had begun because she had taken the time to develop a talent portfolio for each child in her fourth-grade classroom. Plus, Dan talked incessantly about wanting to become a doctor. Because several other children in the classroom appeared to hold the same interest, Mrs. S. invited a local dermatologist to speak to the class. Dan listened intently to the speaker, Dr. M., who spoke of the importance of wearing sunscreen to prevent skin disease. Dan was fascinated and filled out a Science Style Action Information Form to let his teacher know he'd like to learn more about the topic. After meeting with him, Mrs. S. decided his interest was sincere and started to help him plan a Type III activity. She asked him why, if sunscreen works so well to prevent skin disease, more people didn't wear it routinely. Dan's interest was piqued, and he decided to research the prevalence of skin disease in different parts of the world, after which he prepared graphs and charts and analyzed the data. He discovered in very rural areas that the incidence of skin disease was higher. He thought that perhaps the use of sunscreen might have something to do with several factors: exposure to the sun, availability of the product, and knowledge. He met with two experts to confirm his ideas. Then, because his own school was in a very rural area, he went back to Dr. M. to ask if they could conduct a coordinated campaign to raise awareness of the importance of wearing sunscreen and also find a way to distribute free samples of sunscreen. Dr. M. was delighted, and together they worked on the campaign. Dr. M. stopped by the school once a week to confer with Dan, but it was really Dan who took the lead. Dan organized a team of artists in the classroom, including a student who had clear talents in computer graphic design. Together, they developed a character called "Sunny," whose adventures were depicted in a comic book. Sunny's main focus was to teach about the importance of skin care. Meanwhile, Dan also contacted sunscreen product suppliers, who were only too happy to donate hundreds of samples of their product when they found out what Dan was trying to do. The comic book and the sunscreen were bundled in a package together; Dr. M. helped Dan distribute them to all of the local physicians' offices waiting rooms so that children would be given them free of charge. Dan was happy, but wanted to go further, so he asked Dr. M. how they could know they were helping kids wear sunscreen. Dr. M. suggested that conduct a small study in which they interview children who had read the comic and those who had not to determine how frequently they applied sunscreen. They also asked the children if reading the comic made them think about applying sunscreen. When they discovered that the solution seemed to be helping, they were ecstatic!

When reporters at the local television caught wind of the project, they interviewed Dan and Dr. M. The demand for the project grew outside of the local area, spreading to the region and eventually the state. By this point, the two corporate suppliers of the sunscreen became official sponsors and a slicker version of the comic book was produced—although the children's artwork was kept intact. These were distributed statewide and eventually worked their way to a national product.

For as long as she could remember, Carla, a 10th-grade student growing up in the city, had always been interested in math and science. By age 10, she was doing advanced algebra and was well on her way to understanding calculus. She also loved science, especially computer science, and she was frustrated at the thought that one day she'd have to choose between math and science. When her favorite teacher, Mr. D., taught the class how mathematical algorithms could be applied to the scientific world, she became excited at the thought of combining her two interests. Noting her interest, Mr. D. asked her if she would like to complete a Type III activity in this area. Together, they recruited the computer science teacher and a biologist from a local university to work with Carla. The first phase of the project consisted of the team providing Carla with all of the information they could about how math and science work together through technology. Carla excitedly absorbed everything that the team provided her and became more interested in how technology is used to study patterns in genetics. A physician was asked to be on the team, and Carla learned how patients' genetic histories predisposed them to certain outcomes—height, weight, diseases, and more. Gradually, over several months, she was able to write simple algorithms that predicted these outcomes in some patients; primarily she focused on using past data to predict present circumstances. Then it occurred to her that she could use present data to predict future outcomes. By this time, she had graduated to her junior year, but she asked her new math teacher if she could continue the project, working with her previous team.

Carla's attention turned now to something much harder—predicting future outcomes, and she spent her entire junior year struggling with the complexities of the issue. It was frustrating, and one huge stumbling block stood in her way—she didn't have access to some of the supercomputers or large databases necessary to really expand her work. However, after one or two well-placed phone calls, her team was able to connect her with a nearby research institute and mentor who worked in the field. Carla was delighted the first time she stepped into the room with the supercomputer. She sat with her new mentor as he showed her how to access and make sense of the data. She astonished him with the depth of her knowledge, and soon he was talking with her as he would with a colleague. She had a fresh new perspective on how she was developing her algorithms, and together they were able to make huge strides in just a few weeks.

By the time Carla ended her junior year, she had made real breakthroughs in how to analyze genetic data to predict one type of muscular disease that had heretofore been mysterious, and her team encouraged her to enter the Siemens Foundation Competition in Math, Science, and Technology. The high school did not routinely compete; however one or two students had done so in the past, and Mr. D. told Carla she could be a candidate. Carla entered and took home the $50,000 second-place prize.

Teacher as Facilitator in SEM-Science

Unlike in traditional science classes where the teacher plays a central role by planning and implementing prescribed curriculum, the role of the teacher in a SEM-Science setting is more that of facilitator. He or she fulfills this role by assisting students to:

1. *determine their interest* in a topic,
2. *identify the problem* to investigate within the topic,
3. *develop a question* of interest within the topic,
4. develop a Type III investigative activity by *identifying appropriate methodology*,
5. *safely implement* the investigation and *collect data*,
6. encourage *careful analysis and reflection*,
7. *locate an authentic audience* and *showcase* the work, and
8. *evaluate* the work.

Determining Interest

An important consideration in planning activities for the year is that student interest must be taken into account, because the most engaging and effective Type III activities are student-centered. Here is where the total talent science portfolio pays off! By surveying students' interests through the Student Interest Survey for SEM-Science (Handout 4; see p. 44), teachers become familiar with the general interests of their class. However, a second more effective method to determine student interest is to set up early conferences with students. Teachers may question whether time permits such an in-depth, extended activity, but we would argue that the payback is great. Not only do teachers better know and understand their students, but they will find that they relate to the students just a little better after talking with them one-on-one. A suggested list of guiding conference questions is included in Handout 17.

Identifying the Problem Within the Topic

It must be emphasized at this point that, although Type III investigations may include traditional science experiments, they are more than experiments. For example, a high school student may opt to complete a science experiment on whether and how a chemical neutralizes a certain water pollutant, but it's not really a Type III investigation unless the student then puts the results into action. Perhaps the student could patent the product and then meet with a manufacturer to demonstrate its efficacy.

Students may express interest in a topic but have difficulty coming up with ideas for a Type III investigation, and so it may be helpful to think like a scientist by using the questions that scientists routinely ask of themselves and their colleagues about the world around them. Figure 9 lists a few of these "in the field" types of questions that may help students to get started, based on the type of investigation they wish to do.

Scientists' investigations normally fall into one of three categories: observational (sometimes called descriptive), comparative (sometimes called correlational), and experimental. In the first type, observational, scientists are looking to merely understand and describe the characteristics of something. For example, students might want to understand and describe the characteristics of a local river, and they might ask questions such as how deep and wide it is, what type of plant life it sustains, when the water level is highest or lowest, the quality of the water, and more. In descriptive investigations, the traditional 6-W words—who, what, when, where, how, why—work well to generate ideas, but another consideration is if something can be measured and how it should be measured. We add these questions because not all things can be measured. For example, some things are too far away to be measured by students in a classroom (e.g., the characteristics of a distant planet). Also, scientists use numbers to measure many things, but not all things. For example, Charles Darwin found it useful to illustrate small differences between different animals of the same species by sketching them.

A second type of scientific investigation examines the relationships between things. For example, a scientist might explore how age is related to body mass, asking the question, "Is there a relationship between someone's age and his or her body mass?" That is, as someone ages, does body mass increase? Does it decrease? The scientist is not thinking that age causes body mass to increase or

Descriptive
- What do I observe?
- How do I describe it?
- Who is involved with it? Who discovered it? Who is using it?
- What does it look like? What are its parts? What is it like inside? What can be observed about its behavior?
- Where is it located? Where is it used? Where is it in relationship to other things?
- When does it exist or occur? When is it useful or not useful?
- Why did I notice it? Why is it there?
- How does it work or act?
- Can I measure it?
- How do I measure it? With numbers? With words?

Relational
- What are the two characteristics (variables) that I'm trying to understand?
- As there is more of one characteristic, is there less of the other? More of the other? Or is there no relationship?
- What is the nature of the relationship between the two characteristics?

Experimental
- What can I do to change it?
- How do I go about changing it?
- When do I change it?
- What happens if I change it?
- How do I measure it after the change?
- What does the change affect? How?
- What would happen if I didn't change it?
- What would happen if I tried to change it in a different way?

Figure 9. In-the-field questions students may ask in science.

decrease, but she is simply trying to understand what relationship (if any) exists between the two variables of age and body mass. This type of relationship is sometimes called a *correlation*, and the research is correlational research.

A third type of science investigation is the experimental or quasi-experimental research design. In this type of investigation, the researcher tries to hold everything constant while manipulating or changing one or more other variables to see whether it makes a difference in something that is being measured. In this type of research, scientists call the things that are held constant the *control*, or sometimes the *constant* variables. They call the things that are changing or being manipulated the *independent* or *manipulated* variables, and the thing that is being measured as a result of the change is called the *dependent* variable. In this type of investigation, students might ask what they can change and what happens as a result of that change.

Teachers can use the questions that scientists use in the field to encourage students as they identify their interests and connect these interests to an investigable problem. For example, Mrs. D. noticed that Carolina, a bright sixth-grade student, was extremely interested in marine life. Collecting a number of books and websites on the topic, Mrs. D. encouraged Carolina to explore the topic further. Note that marine life is a science topic, not an investigable problem. However, Carolina lived with her family in South Florida, where they owned a small boat. Every Sunday, Carolina would ride out with her family through the intercoastal waters that flowed in and around her small town. There, she saw manatees playing in the water, and she noticed scars on their backs. In the books provided by Mrs. D., she learned that boats often sped through the waters where the manatees resided, scarring them with propellers. Carolina grew more concerned and decided that she wanted to understand the depth of the problem. Mrs. D. reviewed the list of "in the field" questions, and together they decided that Carolina really wanted to do a descriptive study focusing around certain questions. Table 11 presents the questions that Carolina used to guide her investigation, as well as the procedure she used to do so.

After conducting observations for three weekends, Carolina reviewed her data with Mrs. D. Together, they noticed a pattern—most of the collisions with manatees happened during dusk when the light was fading. Carolina also noted that boats returning at dusk appeared to be speeding faster, perhaps in an effort to return safely before nightfall. Together, Carolina and her teacher hypothesized that it was the combination of the fading light and the speed of the boats that created a greater number of incidents with the manatees. They now had identified a problem and could develop a creative solution—one that would encourage boaters to slow down and watch for manatees, especially around nightfall.

At this point, it is necessary to emphasize that there may be two different forms of Type III investigations. One is focused on developing a question and collecting data to develop a solution, similar to the scenario above. Another equally legitimate form of Type III investigation involves developing a model or product that fits a need. For example, let's imagine that a group of middle school students who love to hike on the weekends organize a group outing. They go out and have a great day hiking a local trail, portions of which wind along a lovely boardwalk through a coastal swamp area. Along the way, they see many wonderful exotic plants but have no idea what they are. When they return to school the following Monday, they mention wanting to understand the many plant species they saw. After some discussion with their teacher, two of the students decide to develop a glossy trail guide that can be used by hikers on the local trails. A third

TABLE 11
CAROLINA'S GUIDING QUESTIONS

Question	Procedure
What do I observe?	Carolina observed boats on the intercoastal 8 hours per day, 2 days per weekend, over three weekends. She recorded her observations.
Who is involved with it? What does it look like?	Carolina documented in her observations the size, type, location, and speed of boats, as well as the number and size of the manatees she observed.
What can be observed about its behavior?	Carolina wrote detailed descriptions of the manatees' reactions to the boats.
Where is it located?	On the second and third weekends, Carolina changed her location for observation to determine whether there were similarities or differences in patterns on the intercoastal in terms of boating and manatee behavior.
How do I measure it?	Carolina measured the number, size, and speed of the boats, the number and size of the manatees, and the number of collisions and near-collisions with the boats.

student who is interested in technology would like to work on developing an app that could be downloaded onto local hikers' smartphones. This app would allow hikers to take photos of plants along the trail and upload the photos to the app, which would then return the name and characteristics of the plant species. After working for weeks on these different products, the students contact the management of the local parks and present their products, which are adopted throughout the region.

Handout 18 is included as a way for teachers to encourage students to plan investigations that are focused on the first form of Type III activity—the investigation. It allows teachers such as Carolina's to monitor the progress of these investigations, beginning with the identification of a problem or issue. Students may continue to use this handout to plan and implement their investigations, as well as to collect data and draw conclusions. Handout 19 is included for teachers of students who wish to develop the second form of Type III activity, such as the plant guide. It also allows teacher to monitor students' progress, but the nature of the items is more suited to the development of a product or model. Each of these forms of Type III activities is discussed in more detail below.

Identifying a Problem or Question

All Type III activities are focused on one or more problems or questions of interest. At this point, students will have identified a topic to explore. In the example above, Carolina's problem was that boats were colliding with manatees. She turned this into a two-part question, "Why do boats collide with manatees and what can be done to protect them?" Note that the first part of this question identifies the problem or issue—boats collide with manatees. The second part of the question asks what can be done about it. This second part turns the question into a Type III activity.

Good science questions share certain characteristics. First, they lead to investigations that students may complete in a timely manner and with available resources, either in the classroom or with an instructor or mentor outside the classroom. Helpful parents are an asset, but keep in mind that not every child may be in a home situation in which the parents can help extensively. Another consideration is that the question be researchable using appropriate methodology, as described below.

Good questions are also investigable using methods described below. However, "why" questions are tricky. Carolina started by exploring a "why" question, "Why do boats collide with manatees?" However, Carolina's teacher cautioned her that she could not conclude exactly "why," because there might be other factors that Carolina couldn't observe, such as the physical state or fatigue of the boat owner. She encouraged Carolina to modify her question to include variables that she could directly observe or count. Carolina began to change her "why" question to a series of more observable questions:

› Does time of day make a difference in the number of manatee collisions?
› Does location make a difference in the number of manatee collisions?
› Does speed of the boat make a difference in the number of manatee collisions?

Therefore, by changing the location and time of her observation, she could collect data on frequency of collisions and indirectly get at the "why." Students may use Handout 18 to record their question(s) of interest.

Investigations are normally focused on questions, but the development of a product or model is more focused on identifying a problem that requires a solution, and then developing something that solves the problem. Engineers and investors use this approach daily—from Thomas Edison, who invented the light bulb, to Spencer Silver, who invented the sticky note. In the example with the hikers, the problem was that community members who walked the trail had no guide to inform them of the unique and lovely plant species growing there, and so the product that was needed was a hiking guide and app. Students may use Handout 19 to record their problem statements.

Identifying Appropriate Methodology

As in the general SEM, the teacher's role at this stage in the development of a Type III SEM-Science activity is to guide students in the selection and completion of an appropriate methodology. What types of methodologies lend themselves to Type III activities in science, and how do instructors facilitate the selection and implementation of the "right" approach? First, we must acknowledge that students may take many paths when exploring a topic, and usually there is no one "right" approach. Rather, some approaches lend themselves more naturally than others to the exploration of a topic and the development of a Type III activity, and the selection of a research question is key.

Most questions involve collecting data to understand the underlying issue, and the scientist must consider the type of data to be collected. For example, some scientists use survey methodology. Administering a survey to 500 participants is a good way to understand the ideas of many individuals. However, the survey will not usually yield in-depth information, because most surveys don't contain in-depth questions, as respondents may refuse to complete the survey if they must write lengthy responses. On the other hand, conducting interviews with 10 people is a good way to deeply understand participants' thoughts and ideas at a deeper level, because more time and questioning may be devoted to each participant. Therefore, methodologies lend themselves to purposes—if your purpose is to collect in-depth information, you'll probably want to use an interview rather than a survey. Table 12 presents some typical methodologies that may be used in SEM-Science Type III activities.

Another issue that must be resolved is the type of data that will be collected through these methodologies. Type of data usually involves understanding two main types of information being collected—quantitative versus qualitative information. When a researcher collects qualitative data, he or she is essentially collecting words, and when quantitative data are collected, numbers are involved. For example, the student who conducts a focus group might record the focus group and make notes from the recording and then analyze those notes, looking for patterns in what the participants said. These data will be qualitative in nature. On the other hand, the student who observes and counts the number of manatees and boats is recording numbers, or quantitative information. Qualitative information is generally good for understanding participants' perspectives and for documenting observations or characteristics about something being observed. Quantitative information is generally good for documenting counts or measurements such as frequency and length. Students who use qualitative information will sift through it to look for patterns, whereas students

TABLE 12
TYPICAL METHODOLOGIES USED IN SEM-SCIENCE TYPE III INVESTIGATIONS

Methodology	Purpose	Pros and Cons	Example of Methodology Used in a Type III Investigation
Observations	Used to understand natural behavior or characteristics that occur in an environment.	Pro—Good way to understand behavior and characteristics. Con—Can be time-consuming and difficult to implement; observer may alter the behavior of the observed participants.	A sixth-grade student wants to reduce the number of boat collisions with manatees, and she uses observations of boats and manatees to understand their behavior.
Interviews	Used to collect information on participants' ideas. May be conducted face-to-face or at a distance (e.g., over the phone).	Pro—Good way to collect large amounts of in-depth information. Con—Time-consuming and participants may not always be truthful.	A fourth-grade student is trying to solve the problem of why so many students experience poor nutrition at his school. As part of the project, he interviews two different school administrators to understand their perspective on the situation.
Surveys	Used to collect information from a large group of people, but generally considered less in-depth than interviews. May be conducted face-to-face or electronically.	Pro—Good way to collect information on many participants. Con—Low response rate may bias findings, and information may not be sufficiently in-depth.	A seventh-grade student wants to solve the problem of why the town has no recycling program. As part of the project, she surveys community members to determine whether they would support such a program.
Focus Groups	Used to explore the in-depth ideas of a few people all at once.	Pro—More time-efficient than individual interviews and provides in-depth information. Con—Participants may experience "group-think" and so may not always speak up or be candid about their own ideas.	A fifth-grade student reads about loneliness and anxiety in the elderly. He conducts a focus group with elderly citizens to understand causes and possible ways to address the problem.
Collection and Analysis of Existing Data	Used to explore existing information, such as information on the web, in literature searches, and publicly available database.	Pro—Using existing information is generally easier. Con—May not lead to original ideas.	A 10th-grade student wants to help curb pollution in the area. She uses public online resources to document the growth of contaminants in the local water.
Controlled Investigations	Used to explore natural phenomenon through an experiment in which variables are controlled and the scientific process is used.	Pro—Scientifically rigorous if done well. Con—Requires a level of sophistication and may be difficult to implement.	An eighth-grade student is hoping to develop and publicize an intervention that will improve the effectiveness of study habits in middle schoolers. He designs and tests the intervention's effectiveness using a treatment and a comparison group.

who use quantitative information will use simple descriptive statistics, such as means, medians, modes, frequencies, and percentages to understand the data. Advanced students may also be taught more sophisticated statistical procedures such as correlations and t-tests; today's spreadsheets even have built-in functions to assist with this.

Methodology must be considered in both types of Type III activities—investigations and the development of a product or model. Although the need to gather data may be more apparent in investigatory activities, the need to gather data is also present in the development of a model or product. For example, when considering how to design a basket for a bicycle, students may survey peers to find out the types of items they'd like to carry in the basket. Students may also wish to make in-depth observations of existing products before adding embellishments to create something new. Handouts 18 and 19 provide teachers and students with a table that will allow them to consider different types of methodology and select the most appropriate methodology for the question. Guiding questions are presented for each methodology; but these questions are not meant to be ones that the student will answer on his or her own. Rather, they are meant to guide conversations between the student and the teacher to shape the investigation. A third column in the methodology table allows students to consider materials (e.g., clipboard, paper, pencil, stopwatch) that may be needed while completing the investigation.

Procedure

After selecting one or more methodologies, students may list the steps required for their procedure. We encourage teachers not to skip this step, for the mere act of writing the procedure down will assist students with planning and help them identify potential problematic areas. First, teachers should encourage students to break down their investigation into steps and record these steps in Handouts 18 or 19. Encouraging students to "see the investigation" in their minds as if it were a film is often helpful for students who are struggling to write steps on a page. Some students may question why steps need to be written down, and the answer is that by writing the steps down, the process becomes clearer. After students have tried on their own to write the steps, they should review the procedure with the teacher, who will immediately spot problems or gaps. Fruitful dialogue between teacher and student will allow for the development of an appropriate procedure.

Safety

Safety is another consideration in the science classroom, and it is the science teacher's responsibility to ensure that students are safe, whether they are in the classroom, in a laboratory setting, or sometimes even outside of the classroom collecting data for Type III activities. For example, although Carolina's teacher could not accompany her on her manatee watching expedition, she made sure that Carolina would be accompanied by a parent who would supervise her activities. Table 13 presents some safety concerns for teachers of science who encounter various learning scenarios: in the classroom, out of the classroom on a field trip, and out of the classroom, supervised by a parent or other trusted adult. Students may use Handout 20, "Type III Tidings," to inform parents or guardians of the trip; teachers will wish to use it to ensure that students are safely accompanied. Students may also use Handouts 18 or 19 to record and plan for safety issues they may encounter.

Collecting Data

Students will collect data during their Type III activity that will take the form of numbers and/or words. Here, the two different types of activities—investigations and the product or models—diverge in terms of how data are represented and used. In an investigation, data are recorded and analyzed for patterns and trends that may lead to conclusion. In the development of a model or product, data are analyzed and applied to a solution. A section has been included in Handout 18 to allow students to record the data for their investigations, either on lines or in table form. If using tables, students will need to consider in advance labels for rows and columns. An example of three rows of data for Carolina's manatee investigation is presented in Figure 10.

Of course, if students are collecting an extensive amount of data, they will wish to store their data electronically or perhaps use a science notebook or journal to log data.

Students who are developing a product or model will wish to record their data on Handout 19, under "Development." Note that the boxes contained in the handout allow for careful photos or drawings as the model is being developed. Students may use the observation lines to record facts gleaned from the methodologies they used (e.g., surveys) or their own observations about how the product is developing. Students should be encouraged to document different stages of development as the product or model progresses.

TABLE 13
SAFETY CONSIDERATIONS IN AND OUTSIDE OF THE SCIENCE CLASSROOM

Location	Safety Consideration
In the Classroom	◆ Maintain safe laboratory equipment. ◆ Maintain eye wash in the classroom. ◆ Ensure that students wear safety mask and goggles when handling flammable or potentially harmful chemicals and other items. ◆ Ensure students wear appropriate (nonflammable) clothing and put long hair back or up when handling flammable items. ◆ Try experimental investigations out before teaching them. ◆ Model safety steps prior to allowing students to try the investigations. ◆ Practice safety procedures in the classroom. ◆ Maintain safety equipment such as fire extinguishers. ◆ Safely dispose of harmful chemicals. ◆ Use plastic containers instead of breakable glass containers when possible. ◆ Ensure that electrical appliances (e.g., hotplates) are working and teach students how to handle them appropriately. ◆ Handle biological specimens according to professional guidelines. ◆ Ensure that animals are handled humanely and appropriately. Consider student allergies when bringing animals into the classroom. ◆ Do not allow students to eat or drink during laboratory time. ◆ Ask students to wash hands after handling laboratory materials.
Outside of the Classroom—Supervised Field Trips	◆ Gain parental permission. ◆ Visit the site if possible to understand safety procedures. ◆ Review safety procedures with students ahead of the visit. ◆ Understand health limitations of students who go on the trip (e.g., allergies to bee stings) and bring necessary medical equipment. ◆ Have a plan about what to do if student is lost or if there is another type of emergency.
Outside of the Classroom—Unsupervised Field Trips	◆ Ensure that student will be accompanied by a parent or other safe adult. ◆ Provide documentation of the reason for the investigation.

Date/Time Observed	Location/Speed Limit for Boats	Number of Manatees Observed	Number of Boats	Collisions	Average Speed of Boats
March 21, 2015 3:00–5:00 p.m.	Sewall's Point/ 25 m.p.h.	5	25	1	25 m.p.h.
March 28, 2015 9:00–11:00 a.m.	Sewall's Point/ 25 m.p.h	7	5	0	20 m.p.h.
April 2, 2015 7:00–9:00 p.m.	Sewall's Point/ 25 m.p.h	8	30	2	30 m.p.h.

Figure 10. Carolina's manatee investigation example.

Encouraging Careful Analysis and Reflection

Data collection for an investigation is only the first step in making sense of the problem or answering the question that has been identified. Once students finish collecting data, they will need guidance in learning how to make sense of it. The most important consideration here is that they be reminded again and again that they should eventually answer their question of interest, and to do so, they must look for the answers within the data they collected. They should begin by analyzing the data, exploring for patterns and trends. For example, in the data presented in Figure 10, it is evident that more manatee collisions occurred when more boats were out and when they went faster, generally as evening approached. Fewer collisions occurred during the morning hours, even though more manatee were in the waters. These types of analyses can help to identify the variables at play when trying to understand the problem. In the manatee investigation, the variables that emerged were the number of boats and the speed of the boats. Carolina pondered whether the approaching darkness, coupled with the number of boats and the speed of those boats, distracted drivers from watching out for the manatees.

Students will need to be guided and cautioned at this stage. It would be easy for Carolina's teacher to assure her that she had "found" the answer to her question regarding the causes of boat collisions with manatees, but consider for a moment that other variables may be at play here. Carolina doesn't know whether alcohol consumption may be a factor—she didn't know whether the drivers of the boats had been drinking. She also didn't know whether driver fatigue may play a role. Carolina may be encouraged to state, "Cautious Conclusions," or conclusions that may explain what she saw but that warrant further investigation. She may also be encouraged to think about other possible explanations. Along with these explanations, students should be encouraged to think about "Next

Steps." In other words, what would the next steps be to validating his or her ideas? In Carolina's case, she may wish to investigate the behavior of boat drivers to determine whether alcohol consumption and fatigue could play a role in manatee collisions. She might wish to familiarize herself with how boat drivers obtain their licenses and the rules for alcohol consumption while driving. She might interview a group of boat owners and ask about fatigue and other factors that may play a role. She might ask their opinions about why boats collide with manatees. A section for each of these ideas—"Cautious Conclusions," "Further Explanations," and "Next Steps"—is provided in Handout 18.

Students who are developing a product or model will also need to reflect on the process in terms of what went well and what could be changed. These questions have been included in Handout 19.

Reaching Out: Locating an Authentic Audience

Once students have completed their Type III activities, teachers may be helpful in locating an authentic audience for their work. By "authentic," we mean that the information uncovered by the investigation or the product of the investigation will be useful to someone else outside the classroom. Students are bored by offering information only to each other—it feels artificial because it often is. This presentation to classmates is frequently necessary in school, but one of the most exciting things to do with a group of students is to let them sense how important their work is to someone else—they come alive because it is authentic!

It's often the case that authentic audiences will be regional and outside of the school—for example, a community board—but it's sometimes the case that the audience will be a wider one, depending on the nature of the project. Students need to consider both the nature of the information or product, who might find it useful, and the medium or vehicle for delivering the information. It may be helpful to ask the following questions:

- Who might find the information or product useful?
- Where are they located?
- What would be the best vehicle for delivering the information (e.g., media, book, newspaper, speech)?

Consider the examples in Table 14. These four investigations represent very different purposes and products and so require different types of audiences and vehicles for delivering information. First, think about who will find the information or product most useful. For example, Juan studied flora and fauna in his local community, and then proposed a nature walk to the local parks commission; he

TABLE 14
EXAMPLES OF AUTHENTIC AUDIENCES

Information or Product	Audience and Location	Vehicle for Delivering Information
Juan created a nature walk.	Local parks commission	PowerPoint presentation and handouts to commissioners
Lisa created a working model of an electric car.	Local museum	Letter to museum curators
William studied local sources of water pollution.	Academics	Article in science journal
Allison studied elementary students' knowledge of the importance of brushing teeth properly.	Elementary-school students	Student blog, signs around school, school newsletter, morning broadcast

presented his ideas to the commission through a presentation with handouts. Lisa decided that a museum could showcase her model electric car. She then wrote letters to the curators of a local science museum and sent pictures of the model to accompany the letter; the curators were happy to display the model. On the other hand, William conducted a study regarding a source of local water pollution and decided that academia was the best place to publish his findings and so submitted a research article to a scientific journal. Middle school student Allison found that elementary-aged children didn't brush their teeth properly and so created an advertising campaign to be used at the elementary school, delivering this information through a variety of media.

Students will want to match the type of information or product they have to offer with an appropriate vehicle for delivery, which may include (among others):

- blogs and other social media;
- articles and reports;
- newsletters;
- books;
- speeches;
- letters and e-mails;
- PowerPoint, Prezi, and other types of computer-assisted presentations;
- posters and other types of artwork;
- models;
- media appearances;
- plays; and
- songs.

The teacher's role is to guide students to think about all of the options available, to teach students the necessary Type II skills, and to ease logistics. For example, Lisa, who designed the electric model car above, only thought of displaying the car in the school's library until the teacher suggested contacting the local science museum. Lisa also needed help with letter writing and photographing the model, valuable Type II skills. In a busy classroom, the temptation will be for the teacher to do these things herself. However, it's important that the student should be taught these skills and allowed to do them with guidance. The same rule applies to logistics—have students do for themselves what they can do. A teacher's role is to step in when help is needed. For example, once Lisa had mastered letter-writing, her teacher helped her locate the website for the local science museum. Under a "Contact Me" link, Lisa's teacher guided her to uploading and sending her letter to the curators.

In addition to considering authentic audiences, students will need to develop a communication plan that will allow them to reach those audiences. A communication plan is essentially a list of steps that they will take to communicate with anyone who may be interested in their information or product. Sections to record ideas about reaching out to authentic audiences and communication plans are included in Handouts 18 and 19.

Evaluating the Work

A final key component of a teacher's role in the Type III activity is the evaluation of students' work. The product of an in-depth and research-based instrument development project, the Student Product Assessment Form (SPAF; Renzulli & Reis, 2014) has been used by many teachers through the years and has been shown to have very high reliability and good validity. This means that the form can be trusted to measure what it purports to measure, and it measures it well.

In addition to the SPAF, the SEM-Science Product Evaluation Form in Handout 21 may be used to evaluate students' products in science. The components of this form correspond to the components in students' investigation plans and will allow you to individually assess these components on a scale of 1 (Not Apparent) to 4 (Advanced). Comments may be added to each component and a place to provide overall feedback is included at the bottom of the form. Scores should not be added to obtain totals. Rather, this instrument is meant to provide feedback to the student on the various components of the SEM-Science product.

Summary

Type III activities represent the capstone of the Enrichment Triad, an integral part of the Schoolwide Enrichment Model. Type I exploratory activities expose students to engaging speakers, field trips, books and other resources, and more, and serve as the "hook" for promoting lifelong learning in a discipline. Type II activities provide students with the tools necessary to become creative producers in that discipline. But it is through Type III activities that advanced students are provided the opportunity to become junior practitioners in the field, and this is no small thing. These students will frequently remember completing a Type III activity long after they forget worksheets, and Type III activities have been credited by many students in the past with promoting their early interest in what would eventually become their chosen field. Type III activities are therefore the heart of SEM-Science, but what else is there? Next, we'll explore some of the continuum of services that may be offered outside of the Enrichment Triad to promote students' talents and interests in science.

Name: Date:

HANDOUT 17

SEM-Science Guiding Questions for Student Questions

Teacher Name: ____________________

1. Tell me about yourself. What do you like to do in your free time?

2. Can you remember a book or a movie that you've liked? What was it and why did you like it?

3. What would you like to be when you grow up? Why?

4. If you were grown up and had become a scientist, what type of scientist would you be? Why?

Name: ______________________ Date: ______________

HANDOUT 17, CONTINUED

5. What do you like learning about or doing in science? Why?

____

____

____

____

6. What haven't you liked learning about or doing in science? Why?

____

____

____

____

7. What would you like to learn more about in science this year?

____

____

____

____

8. Is there anything else you'd like to tell me?

____

____

____

____

Name: _______________ Date: _______________

HANDOUT 18

Type III Investigation Plan

1. **Problem to be Solved**

____

____

2. **Question(s) of Interest**

____

____

____

3. **Methodologies—Plan for Collecting Data**

Consider the following and select one or more method to collect your data. Make notes in the notes column as you consider each question.

Method	Questions to Explore	Materials I Will Need
Observations	• What will you observe? • Where will you observe? • How long will you observe? • How many times will you observe? • How will you get there? • Who will be with you? • What types of data will you collect? • How and where will you record what you observe? • Do you have permission to observe? • How will you record and analyze data?	
Interviews	• Who will you interview? • Will you interview them in person, over the phone, or through video conferencing? • How many people will you interview? • What will you ask them that will help you to answer your question? • How long will each interview be? • Do you have permission to interview? • How will you record and analyze data?	
Surveys	• What types of questions will you ask participants (e.g., multiple choice, rating scale, open-ended)? • How many questions do you need to ask? • How will you deliver the surveys (e.g., in person, through the mail, e-mail)? • What will you do about surveys that aren't returned? • How will you record and analyze data?	

Name: Date:

HANDOUT 18, CONTINUED

Method	Questions to Explore	Materials I Will Need
Focus Groups	• Who will you invite to be a part of your focus group? • How many people will you invite? • What questions will you ask? • Will you record the focus group? Do you have permission to record? • How long will the focus group last? Is that too long for participants to remain focused?	
Collection and Analysis of Existing Data	• What data will you collect? • Where is the data? • Do you need permission to collect the data? • How will you store data? • How will you analyze the data?	
Controlled Investigations	• What is your independent variable? • What is your dependent variable? • What are your controlled (or constant) variables?	

4. **Procedure**

   What steps will you take to complete your investigation?

Step	Due By:
1.	
2.	
3.	
4.	
5.	
6.	
7.	
8.	
9.	
10.	

Name: Date:

HANDOUT 18, CONTINUED

5. **Safety Issues**

6. **Data**

Record the data that you collect in the table or on the lines below, or on separate pages.

7. **Reflect**

Explore patterns in your data. What do you notice?

Name: Date:

HANDOUT 18, CONTINUED

Cautious Conclusions: What conclusions can you make? Why?

____

____

____

____

Further Explanations: What else could explain your findings?

____

____

____

____

Next Steps: What would you need to do to validate your findings and explore the problem further?

____

____

____

____

8. **Reach Out**
What audiences might be interested in your data and conclusions? List them below.

____

____

____

____

Name: Date:

HANDOUT 18, CONTINUED

9. Communication Plan

Now the list ways that you will communicate with your audience. Be sure to include dates.

Step	Due By:
1.	
2.	
3.	
4.	
5.	
6.	
7.	
8.	
9.	
10.	

Name: ______________________ Date: ______________________

HANDOUT 19

Type III Product and Model Development Plan

Proposed Product or Model: ______________________

Phase I: Planning the Product or Model

1. **Problem That Model or Product Will Address**

____

____

____

2. **Methodologies—Plan for Collecting Data**
Consider the following and select one or more method to collect your data. Make notes in the notes column as you consider each question.

Method	Questions to Explore	Materials I Will Need
Observations	• What will you observe? • Where will you observe? • How long will you observe? • How many times will you observe? • How will you get there? • Who will be with you? • What types of data will you collect? • How and where will you record what you observe? • Do you have permission to observe? • How will you record and analyze data?	
Interviews	• Who will you interview? • Will you interview them in person, over the phone, or through video conferencing? • How many people will you interview? • What will you ask them that will help you to answer your question? • How long will each interview be? • Do you have permission to interview? • How will you record and analyze data?	
Surveys	• What types of questions will you ask participants (e.g., multiple choice, rating scale, open-ended)? • How many questions do you need to ask? • How will you deliver the surveys (e.g., in person, through the mail, email)? • What will you do about surveys that aren't returned? • How will you record and analyze data?	

Name: Date:

HANDOUT 19, CONTINUED

Method	Questions to Explore	Materials I Will Need
Focus Groups	• Who will you invited to be a part of your focus group? • How many people will you invite? • What questions will you ask? • Will you record the focus group? Do you have permission to record? • How long will the focus group last? Is that too long for participants to remain focused?	
Collection and Analysis of Existing Data	• What data will you collect? • Where is the data? • Do you need permission to collect the data? • How will you store data? • How will you analyze the data?	
Controlled Investigations	• What is your independent variable? • What is your dependent variable? • What are your controlled (or constant) variables?	

3. Procedure

What steps will you take to develop your model or product?

Step	Due By:
1.	
2.	
3.	
4.	
5.	
6.	
7.	
8.	
9.	
10.	

Name: Date:

HANDOUT 19, CONTINUED

4. Safety Issues

____

____

____

____

5. Resources

What resources will you need? List them on the lines below.

____

____

____

____

Plan Approved: ❑ Yes ❑ No

Comments:______________________________________

____

____

____

____

Name: Date:

HANDOUT 19, CONTINUED

Phase II: Development

1. **Development**
   Use the boxes below to draw pictures or insert pictures of your model or product at different stages of development. Use the spaces below the boxes to record observations about each stage.

Date: ______________________ Time: ______________

Observations: ______________________________________

____

____

____

Name: Date:

HANDOUT 19, CONTINUED

Date: ______________________ Time: ______________________

Observations: ______________________

____

____

____

Name: ______________________ Date: ______________

HANDOUT 19, CONTINUED

Date: ______________________ Time: ______________

Observations: ______________________

____

____

____

Name: Date:

HANDOUT 19, CONTINUED

Phase III: Reflection and Reaching Out

1. **Reflect**
   When you finish, think about the process and answer the questions below:
   What did you do well? Why?

   ____

   ____

   ____

   ____

   What didn't you do well? Why?

   ____

   ____

   ____

   ____

   What would you change next time? Why?

   ____

   ____

   ____

   ____

2. **Reach Out**
   What audiences might be interested in your data and conclusions? List them below.

   ____

   ____

   ____

   ____

Name: Date:

HANDOUT 19, CONTINUED

3. **Communication Plan**

Now list the ways that you will communicate with your audience. Be sure to include dates.

Step	Due By:
1.	
2.	
3.	
4.	
5.	
6.	
7.	
8.	
9.	
10.	

Name: Date:

HANDOUT 20

Type III Tidings: A Request for Help

Dear ____________________,

You are receiving this letter because you are a trusted adult in my life. I need help completing my school project that I am calling: ____.

The purpose of this project is to understand ____________________________________.

As part of this project, I need to take a trip to _________________________ in which I will ____.

I hope to collect the following data:

____

____

____

I think that this trip will require approximately ___________ hours ___________ minutes.

Some safety considerations are:

____

____

____

Would you like to accompany me? If so, please sign on the line below and I will return this note to school. If you have more questions, or would like to speak with my teacher, ____________________________, you may reach him or her at _____________________.

Thank you!

______________________________ ______________________________

Signature Printed Name

Student Name: Scored by:

HANDOUT 21

Investigation and Product Evaluation Form

Directions: Rate each of the following by circling the number on the scale provided.

		1 Not Apparent	2 Developing	3 Acceptable	4 Advanced	Comments
Problem or Question	Was the problem clearly connected to the student's final information or product?					
	Was it original?					
	Was it realistic? Could it be investigated or built using materials at hand?					
Methodology	Was an appropriate methodology selected for the nature of the investigation or product?					
Procedure	Was the procedure clearly defined?					
Data Collection	Was the type of data collected appropriate for the question or problem?					
	Were the data or product development organized and presented well?					
Safety	Did the student take safety into consideration?					
	Did the student conduct the procedure safely?					
Reflections–Investigations	Were the student's conclusions related to his or question?					
	Were the conclusions supported by the data?					
	Did the student consider other explanations?					

Student Name: Scored by:

HANDOUT 21, CONTINUED

		1 Not Apparent	2 Developing	3 Acceptable	4 Advanced	Comments
Reflections–Product	Was the student able to describe what went well?					
	Was the student able to describe what didn't go well and make suggestions for improvement?					
Reaching Out	Was the student able to suggest authentic audiences for his or her results?					
Presentation	Was the student able to effectively communicate his or her ideas in the form of a presentation or model to an authentic audience?					
	Taking into account the student's grade level, was the presentation professional in nature?					
Overall	Did the product reflect a commitment of time, energy, and effort?					
	Did the product extend the student's knowledge and skills?					
	Did the product reflect advanced familiarity with subject matter for a student at this grade level?					

Overall feedback:

CHAPTER 7

Additional Components in Science—Beyond Triad

Type I, Type II, and Type III activities make up the heart of SEM-Science, but talented students require additional challenge in the form of curriculum that is both aspiring and appropriately paced, as well as options for specialized programming that extend and enrich their experiences in school. In this chapter, we'll explore a number of these options for students with talents in science.

Curriculum Compacting and Differentiation

Students with aptitude in science frequently do not enter science fields, and this may be in part due to a lack of engagement with the topic throughout middle and high school. We know that understanding science is about more than knowing facts (Donovan, Bransford, & Pelligrino, 1999)—individuals with an expertise in a field must know the facts, understand them within a context, and organize knowledge that allows for retrieval of information and application within the context. Yet, we frequently teach science as an isolated subject consisting of a set of memorized facts. As a result, students don't see the connection that science has to their lives, quickly become bored, and withdraw from the subject.

Instead of teaching facts in isolation, we could be assessing students' levels of knowledge to understand what they know and what gaps in learning may exist. Preassessment is a well-documented tool of learning, and it doesn't need to be painful. Teachers may opt to preassess students' knowledge using formal methods such as quizzes and tests, or they may use more informal methods such as asking students to draw concept maps, make lists, or even discover what they already know through classroom dialogues. The concept map works particularly well in science as a simple way to understand what students know and do not know. For example, when introducing a unit on astronomy, a fourth-grade teacher might provide a list of important words and ask students to write each one in a circle (Figure 11). Students will then connect them with an arrow and label the arrow with a word that makes sense of the two circles that are connected. Students' knowledge of the meaning of each word, as well as their overall familiarity with astronomy, can be easily assessed using this quick and simple method.

Notice that most of the circles in the figure have been connected with arrows, and words on the arrows indicate the direction that the words should be read. For example, the student wrote that the "Sun is a star," which indicates an understanding of the nature of our sun. One circle containing the word *asteroid*, has not been connected to the others, which may indicate that the student doesn't understand what an asteroid is or how it fits into the remaining concepts. Comprehension of scientific concepts may be easily assessed in this manner.

One word of caution about using concept maps—when first teaching how to complete a concept map, it is best to start simple. Provide students with a list of easily understood words such as the following:

- blue
- sky
- sun
- clouds
- white
- moon

Then, show students how to place each word into a circle and connect the words. Emphasize that there is no one "right" way to draw the map, but that students should draw the map to show their best understanding of the words. For example, in the list above, the words *moon* and *clouds* could both be connected to the word *white* and *sky*. A student with a sophisticated understanding might also connect the word *moon* to *blue*, as in a "blue moon."

Once students' levels of knowledge are preassessed, teachers will be able to group them for instruction. These groups are flexible and may change over time, depending on the topic. For example, if fourth-grade student Emily has read everything there is to read about frogs, she may be in an advanced group and

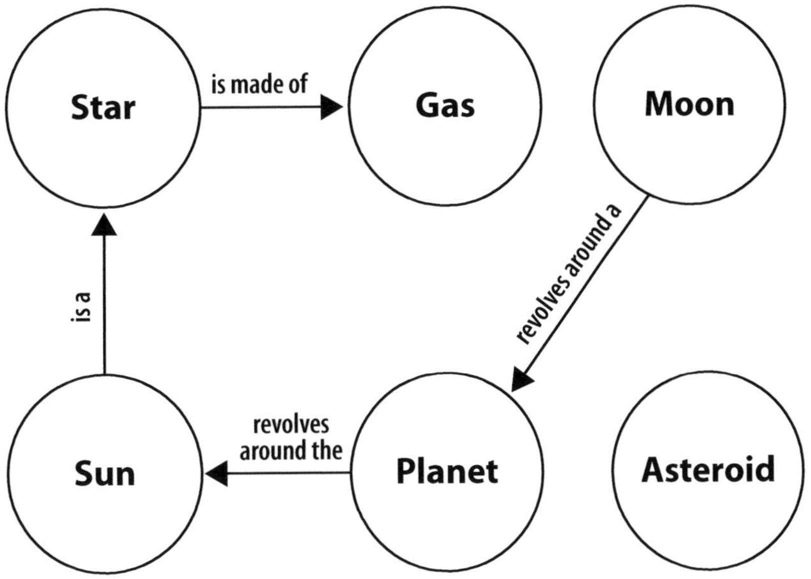

Figure 11. Example of a concept map made by a fourth-grade student.

provided with more advanced content if the class is studying frogs. However, she may be on more of an on-level group if the class is studying chemical reactions and she hasn't acquired an in-depth knowledge of that topic.

Differentiation in science occurs when students have a different understanding of the content of a particular unit of study. For advanced students, teachers will document this understanding and provide more challenging or enriching content to take its place. Frequently in science, this differentiated content will take two forms—more advanced content and/or inquiry-based work. As with the general SEM, students' knowledge of a science topic may be documented using the Compactor. A SEM-Science Compactor has been developed and is presented in Handout 22.

Consider the story of Carlita, a third-grade student who had always been interested in finding and collecting fossils, which were abundant in the area in which she lived in Colorado. Carlita remembered that her obsession with fossils began when she took hikes through the Fossil Discovery Trail at the Dinosaur National Monument not far from her home. When she visited the site with her parents, she noticed many different types of dinosaur fossils in three areas throughout the trail. When she returned home, she read everything she could about dinosaur and other land fossils and learned their names. Carlita's teacher noted her new interest in fossils, and so when the time came to cover the topic in life science, she knew that she would need to differentiate for Carlita.

It is helpful to examine the Next Generation Science Standards (NGSS) at this point, because they may be used as a guide in providing advanced content. The third-grade standard that Carlita's teacher needed to teach was *3-LS4-1: Analyze and interpret data from fossils to provide evidence of the organisms and the environments in which they lived long ago.* Along with the statement, there is a clarification that reads, "Examples of data could include type, size, and distributions of fossil organisms. Examples of fossils and environments could include marine fossils found on dry land, tropical plant fossils found in Arctic areas, and fossils of extinct organisms." Carlita's teacher realized that Carlita was beyond this knowledge, as she had already memorized the names of many land fossils and understood from which plant or animal the fossil derived. However, accompanying many of the standards is an Assessment Boundary, which describes the limits of knowledge appropriate for most of the students at that level. Assessment Boundaries may be used to identify challenging content appropriate for advanced learners. In this case, the Assessment Boundary states, "Assessment does not include identification of specific fossils or present plants and animals. Assessment is limited to major fossil types and relative ages." Carlita's teacher recognized that Carlita knew almost everything there was to know about land fossils but that she had never delved into marine fossils. She decided to differentiate by asking Carlita to research and identify specific marine fossils, providing Carlita with an opportunity to learn more advanced content, but first she needed to document Carlita's knowledge. She asked her to make a list of all of the fossil names she could remember and where they lived. Carlita made a list with three columns—land, sea, and lake—but her land column was much more complete than her sea and lake column. Carlita had provided assessment evidence that Carlita's teacher could use to shape her instruction.

Knowing that Carlita was an advanced reader, Carlita's teacher bookmarked a few websites on freshwater and marine fossils. She brought in a kit containing a variety of these types of fossils and, when the class was doing the primary fossil activity, Carlita worked eagerly to research and identify the water-based fossils. When she finished, she asked her teacher whether she could complete a Type III inquiry-based investigation on land and freshwater fossils in the area. Carlita's teacher documented Carlita's learning using the Compactor in Figure 12, providing evidence of Carlita's level of knowledge and the differentiated activity used to extend her learning.

Student Name: Carlita Marcia		
Name of Lesson or Unit: Freshwater and Marine Fossils		
Next Generation Science Standard: 3-LS4-1: Analyze and interpret data from fossils to provide evidence of the organisms and the environments in which they lived long ago.		
Name It: *What concepts must the student know?* Identify environments of major types of fossils.	**Prove It:** *How do you know the student understands it? Also indicate level of mastery.* Student was able to name many fossils and correctly place fossils into three ecosystems—land, freshwater, marine. However, her knowledge of freshwater and marine fossils is more limited than her knowledge of land fossils.	**Change It:** *What will you do in its place? Why?* Student will research marine and freshwater fossils to identify and place in the correct ecosystems.

Figure 12. Example of a completed Curriculum Compactor in science.

In this example, both advanced content and inquiry-based exploration were used to differentiate learning. It should be noted that although the differentiated activity in which Carlita participated was inquiry-based, it was not a Type III investigation. Carlita went on to develop and implement an inquiry-based Type III investigation in which she explored and documented land and freshwater-based fossils near her home; she used the results of her research to create a display for the children who attended the local natural science museum to learn about fossils.

Within-School Curricular Options

Similar to the general SEM, SEM-Science includes a variety of specialized curricular programming options within schools that allow students to be grouped by ability or interest for the purpose of in-depth instruction. These include cluster groupings, self-contained and pull-out gifted programs, enrichment clusters, challenging secondary school programs such as Advanced Placement (AP) and International Baccalaureate (IB), and acceleration options.

Cluster Groupings and Gifted Programs

Cluster groupings allow teachers to group students with interests and talents in the sciences together within one classroom. Cluster groupings are easily implemented, because they are done at the discretion of the teacher. Gifted programs are more problematic, because they involve district-level decisions and are becoming fewer as the push for heterogeneously grouped classrooms currently dominates in education. However, although they are a rarity nowadays, full-time gifted programs, especially those that focus on science and mathematics, do exist. More common is the "enrichment," or pull-out gifted program, where students stay in a regular classroom for most of the day but are pulled out for enrichment or acceleration opportunities for some portion of time.

Enrichment Clusters

As previously discussed, enrichment clusters form another option for challenging students' interests within the sciences. These interest-based groups are usually self-selected by students and delivered by an adult with an interest and passion for the topic. One of the defining characteristics of enrichment clusters is that the instructor doesn't prescribe the curriculum. Rather, he or she gathers interested students to explore a topic and then allows the idea for a product to emerge from their interests and abilities. Enrichment clusters are usually delivered during a specific time over a period of a few weeks, and science lends itself to a variety of topics appropriate to explore. Administrators and faculty may wish to use Handout 23 to gauge faculty and community interest in particular topics. For more information on enrichment clusters, teachers may wish to refer to *Enrichment Clusters: A Practical Plan for Real-World, Student-Driven Learning* (Renzulli et al., 2014).

AP and IB Programs

Secondary curricular options include AP and IB programs. Following World War II, educators recognized a growing gap between high school and college curricula, and the AP curriculum was created as a way to improve the rigor of high-school academics (College Entrance Examination Board, 2003). Today, millions of secondary students take AP classes and AP exams in dozens of courses, including biology, chemistry, environmental science, physics, computer science, and research (College Board, 2015).

Whereas AP curricula emphasize mastery of content, IB curricula "develop the intellectual, personal, emotional, and social skills needed to live, learn and work in a rapidly globalizing world" (International Baccalaureate Organization, 2015, para. 1). With a growth rate of almost 50% between 2009 and 2014, IB programs are currently offered at almost 4,000 schools worldwide. The aim of an IB curriculum is to teach students to think critically, and the curriculum is divided into four programs: primary years for ages 3–12, middle years for ages 11–16, a general diploma program for ages 16–19, and a newer career-related program for ages 16–19. Science classes are offered in biology, computer science, chemistry, design technology, physics, and sports, exercise, and health science (International Baccalaureate Organization, 2015).

Acceleration

Acceleration provides advanced students with challenging content. Acceleration may take the form of grade or subject skipping and has been shown to be especially effective at improving academic achievement (Colangelo, Assouline, & Gross, 2004). In science, acceleration generally takes the form of exposure to advanced content through specialized courses such as dual-enrollment or other types of college-for-credit courses.

Independent Study

Independent study is yet another option that offers advanced students the ability to study alternate content while other students are mastering the basics. Science readily lends itself to this option, as the independent study can take the form of an inquiry-based or Type III investigation. However, other types of independent studies are possible as well. Consider, for example, the student who pursues knowledge for knowledge's sake, but who does not wish to complete a Type III activity or is not ready for one. He may be prime for researching everything he can about a topic and then presenting his findings to classmates or another interested party. Three important considerations to keep in mind are that the student must be able to work independently, be organized, and be interested in the topic.

Internships, Apprenticeships, and Mentorships

Internships, apprenticeships, and mentorships are good options for providing advanced students with guidance in their fields of interest. We know that immersing students in inquiry-based research is one of the best ways to interest them in the field of science, and these opportunities offer unique occasions for students to conduct advanced research. For example, the Science and

Engineering Apprenticeship Program (SEAP) offers high school students the opportunity to intern in a naval laboratory, working side by side and on-site with researchers (American Society for Engineering Education, 2014). Other programs provide students with a chance to explore engineering opportunities, such as the Bluestamp Engineering Summer Research Program in New York City, Houston, and San Francisco, in which high school students work with engineers to design and build their own projects, taking them from concept to prototype (Bluestamp Engineering, 2015). Appendix B presents a variety of mentor and intern options for students who are interested in science (adapted from Institute for Broadening Participation, 2015).

Additional Programming Options

In addition to within-school curricular options, a number of specialized programming options exist to challenge the advanced student in science. These include specialized schools, virtual schools, and co-curriculars such as clubs and competitions.

Specialized Schools

Specialized schools include a variety of options for using enhanced or challenging curriculum in science; these options include magnet schools, charter schools, and schools that physically exist within other schools. Magnet schools are typically public schools that offer talented students challenging or enriched curriculum, frequently focused on one or more specific subjects. Admission is often competitive, based on criteria that may include interviews, grades, and test scores, although communities may also opt to use an open-enrollment process involving selection of students through a lottery-based system. Magnet Schools of America, a nonprofit professional organization dedicated to promoting excellence in magnet schools, has developed a list of schools that demonstrate a commitment to "high academic standards, innovative curriculum, successful desegregation and diversity efforts, and the consistent delivery of high quality educational services to all stakeholders" (Magnet Schools of America, n.d., para. 1). The list for the 2014 Schools of Excellence, a number of which are oriented toward science and mathematics, may be viewed at http://www.magnet.edu/files/awards/school-of-excellence-list-2014-merit.pdf.

A charter school is a "tax-supported public school that has legal permission (called a charter or contract) from a local or state school board to operate a school, usually for a period of time with the right to review the charter if the school is successful" (Miller-Sadker & Zittleman, 2013, p. 148). Minnesota created the first charter school in the 1990s, and today more than 5,000 of these schools exist. Charter schools vary widely in how effective they are, but frequently they will be given more freedom and opportunity to be creative. Some highly rated charter schools that specialize in science include the Gwinnett School of Mathematics, Science, and Technology in Georgia and the Hawthorne Math and Science Academy in California. The *U.S. News & World Report* ranking of Charter Schools may be found at http://www.usnews.com/education/best-high-schools/national-rankings/charter-school-rankings and data on individual charter schools may be accessed through the National Alliance for Public Charter Schools at http://www.publiccharters.org/get-the-facts/public-charter-schools.

In an effort to downsize and improve curricular offerings, some locales are opting to offer a school-within-a-school model. In this model, a separate school is established within the facilities of an existing educational facility. This separate school will usually establish and maintain a separate mission, its own governing body, and its own curriculum. Frequently, these schools focus on science and related subjects. For example, the School of Environmental Science and Technology housed in South Grand Prairie High School in Grand Prairie, TX, and the Academy of Science and Medicine housed in Mainland High School in Daytona Beach, FL, both focus on subjects related to science. Local school district websites will list whether they offer this option.

Virtual Schools

At virtual schools, students take courses online through a course provider. One of the most established providers is The Virtual High School. Fully accredited and with more than 15 years of experience at delivery of online content, The Virtual High School currently offers middle school and high school STEM, AP and honors, and gifted and talented courses, which are offered during the summer as well as during the regular school year. Courses are offered in a wide variety of areas, ranging from AP Biology to Engineering for Sustainable Energy (The Virtual High School, 2014). At The Virtual High School and other virtual schools, students are free to learn at their own pace and to explore course offerings not normally offered at more traditional schools.

Co-Curriculars for Enrichment—Clubs and Competitions

In addition to curricula and activities that usually take place during the school day, co-curricular opportunities for enrichment take place before or after the school day, or sometimes on the weekends. A number of co-curricular opportunities exist in science, and they frequently take two forms—clubs and competitions. These opportunities serve to jump-start students' interests in a particular area. For example, the middle school girl who doesn't know she's interested in astronomy may, on a whim and because it fits into her schedule, join an astronomy club. During an outing to observe stars through the club's powerful telescopes, she may become intrigued and want to know more. A lifelong passion may be born! Table 15 presents co-curricular options for students who are interested in science.

Summary

Parents and teachers may explore a wealth of opportunities for students with interests and talents in STEM. These opportunities range from in-school programs, curricula, and activities, to specialized and virtual schools. Together, these options provide a continuum of services that will maintain students' engagement with learning, deepening their content knowledge and skills while preparing them for future careers in science.

Another aspect of preparing students for the future is teaching them to how to use technology and how to prepare to work in a world with future technologies that are unimaginable today. In the past 50 years, we've seen the invention of a host of new technologies that have changed the landscape of our world, and the next chapter will explore how to integrate some of these technologies into the science classroom.

TABLE 15

CO-CURRICULAR OPPORTUNITIES IN SCIENCE

Age	Title	Website Address	Description	Grade Level
All Ages	The DuPont Challenge	http://thechallenge.dupont.com	Online science essay competition	K–12
	Exploravision	http://www.exploravision.org	Sponsored by NASA and NSTA	K–12
	FIRST Robotics Competition	http://www.usfirst.org/roboticsprograms/frc	Engineering competition where students are tasked with creating a robot to perform certain tasks	K–12
	Future Problem Solvers	http://www.fpspi.org	Stimulates critical and creative thinking skills	4–12
	NASSP National Advisory List	http://www.nassp.org/awards-and-recognition/nassp-national-advisory-list	Lists student contests and activities for the school year	K–12
	Odyssey of the Mind	http://www.odysseyofthemind.com	Focuses on creative problem solving	K–College
	Science Olympiad	http://soinc.org	Regional, state, and national science competition	K–12
High School	U.S. National Chemistry Olympiad	http://www.acs.org/content/acs/en/education/students/highschool/olympiad.html	National team-based chemistry competition	High school
	Google Science Fair	https://www.googlesciencefair.com/en	Science fair hosted by Google	Ages 13–18
	Intel International Science and Engineering Fair	http://www.intel.com/content/www/us/en/education/competitions/international-science-and-engineering-fair/event-summary.html	International science fair	High school
	Intel Science Talent Search	http://www.intel.com/content/www/us/en/education/competitions/science-talent-search.html	Distinguished precollege competition open to rising high school seniors; focuses on research	High school seniors
	Junior Science and Humanities Symposia	http://www.jshs.org	Individual students compete for scholarships and recognition by presenting the results of their original research efforts before a panel of judges and an audience of their peers	High school
	USA Biology Olympiad	https://www.usabo-trc.org	Biology competition	High school

TABLE 15, CONTINUED

Age	Title	Website Address	Description	Grade Level
Middle School	eCybermission	https://www.ecybermission.com	Web-based competition	6–9
	Broadcom MASTERS	https://student.societyforscience.org/broadcom-masters	Science fair held in Washington, DC	Middle school
	Christopher Columbus Awards	http://www.christophercolumbusawards.com	Students use the scientific method to identify a community need and write a grant to address it	Middle school
	Rubber Band Contest	http://rubberbandcontest.org	Students design and create a working invention that incorporates at least one rubber band	5–8
	You Be the Chemist Challenge	http://chemed.org/ybtc/challenge/home.aspx	Chemistry competition	5–8
	Young Scientist Challenge	http://www.youngscientistchallenge.com	Video submission science competition	Middle school
	Humans in Space Art	http://www.lpi.usra.edu/humansinspaceart	Art competition where students are tasked with creating a descriptive artwork of humans in space	Ages 10–18
Secondary	National Science Bowl	http://science.energy.gov/wdts/nsb	Question and answer competition for teams of four students	Secondary
	Team America Rocketry Challenge	http://www.rocketcontest.org	National rocketry challenge	Secondary
Elementary	Camp Invention	http://campinvention.org	Nationally recognized, nonprofit summer elementary enrichment program	Elementary
	The Kids' Science Challenge	http://www.kidsciencechallenge.com	Students submit experiments and problems for a panel of scientists to solve	3–6
	NSBE KidZone Elementary Science Olympiad	http://www.nsbe.org/NSBE-Jr-Archive/Competitions-and-Contests/Kid-Zone.aspx	Teams test their science skills in 18 different events at the National Society of Black Engineers (NSBE) National Convention	3–5
	Scientists in School	http://www.scientistsinschool.ca/contests-events.php	Presents a series of challenges for elementary students	Elementary

HANDOUT 22

SEM-Science Compactor

Student Name:		
Name of Lesson or Unit:		
Next Generation Science Standard (NGSS):		
Name It: *What concepts must the student know?*	**Prove It:** *How do you know the student understands it? Also indicate level of mastery.*	**Change It:** *What will you do in its place? Why?*

Name: Date:

HANDOUT 23

Enrichment Cluster Sign-Up Sheet

Directions: Examine the topics below. Print your name in the column next to a topic if you would be willing to lead an enrichment cluster on the topic. Feel free to suggest a topic for which you have an interest and ability under "Other."

Topic	Name
Plants	
Animals	
Microscopic Life	
Electricity	
Motion	
Hot and Cold	
Matter	
Matter Transformations	
Chemical Reactions	
Astronomy	
Origins of the Universe	
Extraterrestrial Life	
Rock Collecting	
Weather	
Oceanography	
Machines and How They Work	
Model-Making	
Light and Photography	
Other	

CHAPTER 8

Keeping Up With Technology

If you had peeked through a window in an elementary school classroom in 1960, you might have seen neat desks lined up in careful rows. The teacher would probably have been lecturing in front of a chalkboard, and students would have been sitting at desks on which lay paper, pencils, and perhaps an open textbook. Those students grew up, graduated, and entered the world just as the information age was dawning. They saw the advent of the personal computer, VHS and DVD recording devices, and sophisticated and powerful software that allowed them to use the computer in ways that their teachers never dreamed of in the 1960s. Lately, these same students as adults have witnessed computers becoming increasingly more powerful, affordable, and smaller, wrapped in mobile packages—MP3 players, mobile tables, and cellphones.

The International Society for Technology in Education (ISTE) has put forth the case that societies are changing and so expectations about the type of technological knowledge and skills students must master is rapidly changing. The teachers of those students in the 1960s could neither have imagined nor prepared their students to work with cellphones, and today's teachers are in a similar situation. We can't predict how technology will evolve, but we can prepare students to work with today's cutting edge technology to better equip them to cope with the rapid development that likely lies ahead.

Technology is changing, and educators must lead. Luckily, guidelines exist for the thoughtful integration of technology into the curriculum. For example, the ISTE has established standards for teachers, students, administrators, and more, available at http://www.iste.org/standards. These standards guide the meaningful integration of technology into curriculum. In terms of science, some researchers (Flick & Bell, 2000) have suggested that technology needs to be introduced in relation to science content, and not as gadgets that are disconnected or not meaningfully connected to the knowledge and skills students need to acquire. Sure, technology can be exciting, but more importantly, technology is a lifelong tool that science learners need to be able to use at increasingly sophisticated levels.

The meaningful integration of advanced technology into science curricula is even more important for students with interests and abilities in science for a number of reasons. First, technology frequently allows these students to comprehend science in a way that's impossible without it. For example, students who experience a virtual trip into space through their computers are experiencing something that, at the present time, they cannot experience without the assistance of technology. Next, technology can be the "hook" that captures and maintains students' interest in science. Watching a student whose eyes light up the first time they use a microscope connected to a projector will convince even the most skeptical teacher that technology can be engaging. Finally, if we are to prepare these students for future careers in science fields, it only stands to reason that they should be prepared to step into those careers with solid skills working with the tools of the field.

We have witnessed an explosion of technology in the past decade. With the advent of mobile devices such as smartphones and tablets, schools have begun to realize and harness the potential of these powerful computing devices. Approximately 85% of districts have implemented a "bring-your-own-device" policy that allows students to transport these personal devices from home, and more than half encourage the use of the devices for educational purposes in the classroom (Godfrey, 2013). Students routinely search the Internet to locate information and download apps that are useful to learning. More technology exists than ever, but what are the different kinds of technology available, and how may they be put to best use in the science classroom?

Types of Technology

Besides the websites mentioned in previous chapters, a number of specialized types of technology may be used by teachers to enhance students' learning. These include app technology, clickers, cloud computing, concept mapping, modeling software, probeware, specialized SEM software known as GoQuest, and simulations.

App Technology

With the advent of smart technology, portable devices are becoming integrated into the classroom and harnessed as a resource for teaching. "Bring-your-own-device" policies are becoming more commonplace at school and may be used to engage students in science (Heilbronner, 2014). Table 16 presents examples of engaging apps that are available across multiple formats (e.g., Apple and Android) that are either free or available to download for a small cost, usually under $1.

In addition, students may use apps in the place of scientific instruments. For example, virtual stopwatches, rulers, decibel meters, and levels abound, and teachers may use these in place of physical instruments or to enable students to create interesting initial investigations that may spark an interest in a topic (for more information on this type of investigation, see Heilbronner, 2014, and Renzulli, Heilbronner, & Siegle, 2010).

Clickers

Instructional clickers are small hand-held devices that students use to interact with the instructor and the materials in various engaging ways, including recording their responses to teachers' questions, participating in opinion polls, and more. Students' responses are transmitted wirelessly to a receiver that contains specialized software that enables students' answers to be aggregated or disaggregated and displayed in various ways. For example, an instructor might ask her class to identify the age of the Earth by selecting the correct answer from among four choices. Students click a key on their units and their responses are transmitted, aggregated, and projected onto a SmartBoard in the form of a bar graph.

By using clickers in the science classroom, teachers can raise the level of participation and engagement in learning. Teachers may also use clickers to diagnose students' level of skill or knowledge regarding a particular topic. A few companies have also designed software that students may download and use on mobile devices that functions in the same manner but eliminates the need for a physical clicker.

TABLE 16
EDUCATIONAL APPS FOR SCIENCE CLASS

Area	Title of App	Description
Astronomy	Britannica Kids: Solar System	An interactive reference guide for information about the solar system.
	Cosmic Cubs	Gives students the opportunity to create their own stories about adventures into space.
Biology	Project Noah	Students upload photos to help with global research missions.
	Solve the Outbreak	Developed by the Center for Disease Control and Prevention (CDC), the app places students in the role of disease detectives.
Earth Science	Britannica Kids: Volcanoes	Students learn the science behind the devastating power of volcanoes through impressive photos and engaging interactive games and activities.
	Kid Weather	Designed by a 6-year-old boy and his meteorologist father, the app encourages exploration of the science behind weather through a series of interactive games, real-time weather information, use of avatars, and more.
Physical Science	Cat Physics	Users control a ball by passing it around from cat to cat and learn the basics of momentum and force.
	Crazy Machines	Provides students with the opportunity to build machines and experiment with them.
General Science	BrainPOP	Derived from the original BrainPOP website, the app offers one free movie per day and more on a subscription basis.
	Science 360	Designed by the National Science Foundation and geared toward older students, the app presents a series of "stories" on a range of topics in science.
	Sid's Science Fair	Based on the popular television show, the app encourages exploration of inquiry and the scientific method.

Cloud Computing

In cloud computing, data are stored "in the cloud," or online so that users may access the data remotely. This remote access offers several advantages to teachers and students. It enables students to access their own work from home or another location, and it allows work to be shared for the purposes of communication and collaboration. Several good sites exist that can store students' data, including Google and wikis. Google has created a suite of products that will allow students to work collaboratively in real time on documents (Google Docs), surveys (Google Surveys), and presentations (Google Slides). For example, students might study the rainforest and use Google Docs to make a collaborative list of their findings from home.

Wikis are another online cloud computing resource. Wikis function like editable web pages, and science teachers may wish to use them to store resources (e.g., articles, media, websites) for their students to access. Teachers may even use wikis to differentiate work (Heilbronner, 2013a). A number of good wiki sites exist, and authorize free use for educators, including PB Wiki (http://www.pbwiki.com) and Wikispaces (http://www.wikispaces.com).

Concept Mapping

Concept mapping, a process in which students write a word representing a concept in a box and then connect those boxes with arrows that are labeled with linking words, helps students to develop an understanding of scientific concepts and helps teachers to assess students' knowledge of those concepts, both before and after instruction. Although science concept maps may be created on paper, software such as CMap Tools (http://cmap.ihmc.us) or Inspiration (http://www.inspiration.com/visual-learning/concept-mapping) may be more engaging because they allow students to embed sounds and visuals such as pictures and videos into their maps. Editing is also easier with virtual maps.

Modeling Software

The study of science is replete with the study of complex systems, such as ecosystems, the water cycle, and biological systems of the body. Advanced modeling software allows students to understand the dynamics of complex systems by building them and modifying them to study the impact of these modifications. Students develop content knowledge and general process skills while doing so (SciMathMN, 2015). Modeling software such as Model-It and Starlogo Nova are examples of this type of software.

Probeware

Sophisticated probes connected to computers are used in the science classroom to collect and display data simultaneously, advancing students rather quickly into the analysis phase. A variety of data may be collected by probes, including temperature, pH, water turbidity and dissolved oxygen, light, magnetism, and more. The probe is usually a handheld device that the student manipulates and is connected to a computer that collects and stores data from the probe, often while providing real-time graphic and tabular displays.

GoQuest™

GoQuest™ (Compass Learning, 2013; http://renzullilearning.com) is the newest component of the SEM. It is an interactive online program that aids in the implementation of SEM by matching student interests, expression styles, and learning styles with a vast array of enrichment educational activities and resources, designed to enrich gifted and high-potential students' learning process. Using GoQuest™, students explore, discover, learn, and create using the SEM married to the most current technology resources independently and in a safe environment. GoQuest™ consists of a series of services that represent the various components of SEM.

The Renzulli Profiler is an interactive assessment tool that identifies students' talents, strengths, interests, and preferred learning and expression styles to provide a comprehensive student learning profile. The Portfolio is a computerized assessment tool, creating a unique profile for each student. It consists of carefully selected, user-friendly, research-based questions related to a student's particular interests. The system assesses students' interests in 13 major categories, including performing arts, writing and journalism, mathematics, history, fine arts, sciences, athletics and sports, photography/video, social action, business, technology, literature/reading, and foreign languages.

Students' expression styles are also assessed, whether they are writing, oral debates, stage performance, sculpture, dance, or a host of other expressive techniques; the student shares how he or she most enjoys interacting with the world. The Portfolio considers 10 specific expression styles: written, oral, hands-on, artistic, audiovisual/display, dramatic, service, technological, musical, and commercial.

GoQuest™ also assesses learning styles or the ways students like to learn new information ranging from individualized study to large group learning, from paper-based review to digital technology, focusing on nine learning styles: lecture, computer-assisted instruction, discussion, peer tutoring, group work, learning games, technology, simulations, and independent studies. Students answer questions about their interests, learning, and product styles in 30–50 minutes, and the Portfolio produces an accurate, printable assessment of each student's interests, abilities, and how that individual best learns. Even better, the Profiler reflects the world of learning from the *students'* perspective, not necessarily that of their parents or teachers. This makes it possible to provide enrichment based on the Enrichment Triad Model with optimum effectiveness and efficiency. By representing the student's view, the Portfolio assessment becomes a major productivity tool for teachers—placing them literally months ahead in their efforts to understand each child's learning style(s), and to be able to respond to and incorporate those styles as part of an effective learning plan.

The GoQuest™ database includes thousands of carefully screened, grade-level appropriate, child-safe enrichment opportunities that are regularly monitored, updated, enhanced, and expanded at a rate of more than 500 per month. The GoQuest™ database provides teachers with a vast storehouse of differentiated enrichment materials and resources for students with varying ability levels, interests, learning styles, and preferred styles of expression. To truly individualize and differentiate for students of various needs, teachers using GoQuest™ have easy access to an unlimited supply of enrichment activities and resources that make such differentiation possible. The databases are organized into 14 separate categories, representing a wide range of educational activities. These include: virtual field trips, real field trips, creativity training activities, training in critical thinking, independent study options, contests and competitions, websites based on personalized interests, high-interest fiction books, high-interest nonfiction books, how-to books for conducting research and creative projects, summer program options in special talent areas, online activities and research skills, research skills, videos, and DVDs. All enrichment database entries are carefully researched by GoQuest™ educational specialists, screened for grade-level applicability, and coded as one of the 14 enrichment categories. Elements of each category are then matched to students' top three choices of interests, learning styles, and product styles, providing each student with a unique personalized selection of enrichment opportunities. The search automatically links each student's Profile with the enrichment database to generate a customized list of activities designed to appeal to that student's grade level, interests, and abilities, as well as his or her learning and expression styles.

A secondary self-directed search enables students and teachers to enter a set of one or more self-selected keywords to locate specific database entries from their own individual activity list or from the entire database. This feature is particularly useful for selecting a particular topic for project work or for in-depth study. A global search capability enables students and teachers to access the entire enrichment database, across all interests, expression styles, learning styles, or even grade levels. This permits students with above-grade capabilities to locate and pursue new activities and threads of interest, all within the safety of a prescreened information environment. It also helps teachers identify possible projects and other curriculum enhancements within the same space their students explore. The GoQuest combined search facilities offer children an extensive, expanding menu of learning opportunities, and offer teachers a new and valuable resource for their classroom preparation.

The Total Talent Portfolio provides a complete record of students' online learning activities and academic progress and an online portfolio to save students' best work. The Talent Portfolio enables students to create and post writings, Internet links, images, and other work on projects or areas of interest.

The Wizard Project Maker is an online project-management tool that helps students to create their own high-interest projects and store them in their own Talent Portfolio. More than 200 Super Starter Projects are being added to the Project Maker to enable students to begin the process of doing projects on a small-scale, short-term basis that may later enable them to initiate and complete projects more independently.

GoQuest also offer a series of management tools for teachers, administrators, and parents, designed to help follow individual students' learning progression, analyze group usage patterns, and formulate lesson plans and classroom organization. GoQuest features a collection of administrative reports designed to help make the process of enriching each student's learning process more efficient. These tools enable teachers, parents, and other mentors to learn more about their students and to make grouping and enrichment easier. Reports include printable listings of individual and group interests, as well as individual and group summaries of student expression styles and learning styles. Also available are teacher learning maps for enrichment differentiation activities, downloadable enrichment projects, downloadable creativity training activities, background articles by leading educational practitioners, lesson plans for using the GoQuest effectively, and outstanding websites for teachers.

These components provide both students and teachers with unique educational experiences, directly suited to each individual's learning profile, while simultaneously giving parents insights about their child's enrichment needs. GoQuest also helps all teachers better understand and know their students and thus meet their diverse needs. Perhaps the most significant aspect of GoQuest is its emphasis on a student's strengths, celebrating and building upon students' academic abilities, and interests, in the tradition of SEM. This web-based online program matches students' interests, learning styles, expression styles, abilities, and grade level to thousands of opportunities designed to provide enriched, challenging learning. It gives teachers a virtual equivalent of multiple "teaching assistants" in their classrooms—each and every day—to implement the SEM.

Teachers can also access exciting websites to help their own teaching and download creative activities to use in their classroom. They can monitor students' progress by accessing their profiles and viewing all of the activities and assessments that they have completed. Teachers using this system can even submit their own ideas for activities and interact with other teachers, enrichment specialists, curriculum coordinators, and administrators from around the country. Finally, parents can view their child's progress, his or her profile, and his or her choice of enrichment activities and projects.

Simulation Websites

Instructional games may be used to teach a variety of science process skills, especially those that relate to problem solving. Simulations are a specific type of instructional game. As previously discussed, simulations place students in situations that in real life may be impossible or dangerous to be in. For example, simulation software may allow students to rocket through space or journey back in time to encounter dinosaurs. A number of excellent dissection experiences exist on the web. For example, the software Froguts allows students to perform virtual dissections of a frog, cow eye, squid, starfish, owl pellet, and more, and at the University of Colorado's pHet site (https://phet.colorado.edu), teachers may select simulations by grade level across different strands of science. Table 17 presents examples of these types of websites.

Summary

Rapid advances in technology require us to prepare students to be competitive in the global market by exposing them to the most cutting-edge ideas and tools. Technology such as apps, probes, specialized software, and cloud computing keep learning fresh and fun, engaging students in a powerful way. These tools also enable students to acquire the skills and knowledge that will form the basis for even more advanced skills they will need in the future. For science, perhaps the most important consideration is that technology serves as the lifeblood of the discipline. Scientists use technology daily to explore the world around us and the heavens above us. Encouraging students to do the same enables them to understand their own world and makes learning meaningful and relevant.

TABLE 17
WEBSITES CONTAINING SIMULATION ACTIVITIES IN SCIENCE

Title of Website—*Website Address* **Description**
Dissections
Froguts— *http://www.froguts.com* • Students virtually dissect a cow eye, frog, owl pellet, fruit fly, and more. Subscription required.
Virtual Own Pellet Dissection— *http://kidwings.com/nests-of-knowledge/virtual-pellet* • Students virtually dissect an owl pellet.
Virtual Cow Eye Dissection— *http://www.exploratorium.edu/learning_studio/cow_eye* • Students virtually dissect a cow eye.
Virtual Frog Dissection— *http://www.mhhe.com/biosci/genbio/virtual_labs/BL_16/BL_16.html* • Students virtually dissect a frog.
Field Trips
360 Cities— *http://www.360cities.net* • Contains one of the largest collections of high definition panoramic images from locations around the world.
Arctic— *http://www.polarhusky.com* • Endorsed by the National Science Foundation, the site pairs the excitement of following long dog-sled journeys with actual research and an inquiry-based curriculum.
Smithsonian National Museum of Natural History— *http://www.mnh.si.edu/panoramas* • Sponsored by the Smithsonian Institute, the site allows users to virtually navigate through its National Museum of Natural History and explore the exhibits.

CHAPTER 9

Conclusion

Blending Standards With Opportunities for Creative Teaching

In the first chapter, we described a case study that exemplified how one teacher was able to personalize the learning process for a student (Maria) while also taking account of the Next Generation Science Standards. We believe that these standards are an important step forward for improving instruction in science. At the same time, however, we also believe that teachers must have the commitment and skills to infuse high engagement enrichment activities into any and all standards-driven instruction. Science instruction, especially for our most able students and future scientists, should not be designed to "standardize" them! Rather, the kinds of teaching that will produce the next generation of creative and productive scientists must respect the standards and *also* provide the kinds of personalized learning that promotes high engagement and a passion for producing the applied and creative knowledge we described in the first chapter. The rationale for why this blending of prescribed instruction and enrichment experiences is important can best be illustrated by the following story.

As a 15-year-old schoolboy, Sir John Gurdon, winner of the 2103 Nobel Prize in medicine for his pioneering work in cloning stem cells was told that a career in science was "ridiculous." He keeps the following report written by one of his teachers over his desk to this day.

> His work has been far from satisfactory. His prepared study has been badly learnt and several of his test pieces have been torn over. One such piece of prepared work scored 2 marks out of a possible 50. His other work has been equally bad, and several

> times he has been in trouble, because he will not listen, but will insist on doing his work in his own way. On his present showing this is quite ridiculous. If he can't learn simple Biological facts he would have no chance of doing the work of a scientist, and it would be sheer waste of time, both on his part, and those who would have to teach him. I believe he has ideas about becoming a scientist: on his present showing this is quite ridiculous.

We have been asked on numerous occasions how teachers can do the kinds of teaching recommended in this book and, at the same time, adhere to the pressures that externally imposed standards and high stakes testing are placing on the instructional process. If a concern for John Gurdon's interests and especially his learning styles were taken into account, perhaps the above report would never have been written, or it might have at least commented on a person of promise who could and should been challenged in ways that were more accommodating to his style of "doing his work in his own way." High levels of engagement don't necessarily result from memorizing biological facts or adhering to the homogenized instruction that is typically the norm in so many of our standards-driven classrooms. If there is one thing that we know about improving the effectiveness of the learning process, it is that high engagement results in both high achievement and much more enthusiastic and joyful learning. One of the biggest challenges facing the education of our highest potential students is overcoming boredom by balancing the need to provide students with enrichment opportunities within the context of an overly prescribed or required curriculum. The emergence of the standards-based movement, coupled with the almost overpowering influence of standardized testing, has had the effect of squeezing highly engaging enrichment activities out of the curriculum. Many teachers have become so accustomed to the regimen brought on by the demands to meet standards that they are using overly prescribed material and don't know how to deviate from it. They also become dispensers of the type of received knowledge that was described in Chapter 1 of this book. Few would argue that standards-driven curriculum is not important; however, research has clearly and unequivocally shown that high engagement enrichment experiences do in fact, contribute to higher achievement scores *and* they also make school more meaningful and enjoyable for students (Dotterer & Lowe, 2011; Greenwood, 1991; Reyes, Brackett, Rivers, White, & Salovey, 2012; Wang & Holcombe, 2010).

In this chapter, we present a strategy that teachers can use for achieving some balance between the required curriculum and a way of infusing enrichment activities into standards-driven material. Teachers who have used this technique have commented about how it has made them feel more creative about their teaching and more like professionals rather than mere purveyors of highly prescriptive received knowledge. This approach, which we simply call Curricular Enrichment Infusion, can be employed to make science instruction at all levels come alive by following the steps described in the following section.

Enriching Science Curriculum Through an Infusion-Based Approach

An infusion-based approach simply means that teachers will:

- review and **select** highly engaging enrichment-based activities related to particular topics,
- **inject** them into the curriculum to make the topics more interesting, and
- provide support and encouragement for individuals and small groups who would like to **extend** their pursuit of the enrichment activities.

A few examples will illustrate how the infusion process works.

A high school AP Physics teacher provided Type I Enrichment experiences by inviting a local physicist to speak and using DVDs to expose students to the various types of professional responsibilities of physics. When students became interested in global positioning system (GPS) devices as a result of one of the presentations, the teacher obtained a GPS and taught the students how to use this instrument (Type II Enrichment). At this point, he told the class that they could work individually or in small groups to design a yearlong project using the GPS as well as other equipment. The only condition was that the students were required to show how the content of each science unit of study covered in their class could be applied to their project. One group decided to study the topography of their area by launching a weather balloon carrying a platform that contained a video camera, a GPS tracking device, and various weather data-gathering instruments. Through this Type III Enrichment process, they recorded the journey, prepared topographical maps, and analyzed data about temperature, air pressure, and humidity. Final research papers required information about how the principles and concepts they studied in their physics class applied to their project, making learning more relevant and meaningful.

Another example involved a sixth-grade science teacher who took her class on a field trip to the local science museum (Type I). There, students were engaged with learning about the latest designs and uses for drone technology, and later, the teacher challenged students to develop a new type of drone and relate it to something that had never been done before (Type II). Students developed ideas for the use of drones and, using a set of criteria that they developed, evaluated each idea (Type II). They selected one for further development. The teacher brought in an expert on drone technology to work with students and refine the concept so that ultimately, these students were able to actually build a functional drone (Type III) that could fly short distances from one location to another, acting as a sort of retrieval mechanism for items around the house.

As a final example, consider the case of the third graders who became engaged with learning about birds. After a trip to a local nature museum (Type I), their teacher struggled with how to extend this enthusiasm, but then used a brainstorming technique to develop ideas for her class for further exploration of birds. She was able to develop a number of activities (see Figure 13) that allowed students to learn about the topic. Students self-selected the activities they wished to pursue, and for a week studied the topic of birds in this manner. With their imaginations captured, they went on to conduct a more in-depth investigation about why particular species of birds were not returning to the area after their winter migration. Students advocated for a piece of open land to be devoted to a bird sanctuary, taking their case before the local community council. After some time, they won their case and even went on to provide a design for the sanctuary (Type III). In this example, creative infusion worked to capture the hearts and imaginations of the students, allowing them to springboard into more meaningful investigations.

The Role of Technology in Finding Resources for Infusion

This engagement and infusion approach works because teachers have the tools to implant highly engaging material into the standards-based curriculum and to use technology to locate what we described earlier as Just-In-Time (J-I-T) Knowledge that is relevant to their projects—exactly what adult researchers do as they go about the investigative and creative processes. The advent and easy access to the larger world of knowledge has provided opportunities to make formal learning a different process than it was a decade or two ago. Today's young people are digital learners and emerging masters of interactive media technology, using cell phones and handheld devices regularly to access J-I-T information (e.g., movie, bus, and TV schedules; sports scores; restaurants, etc.). Traditional ways of learning, even under the best of circumstances, cannot compete with students

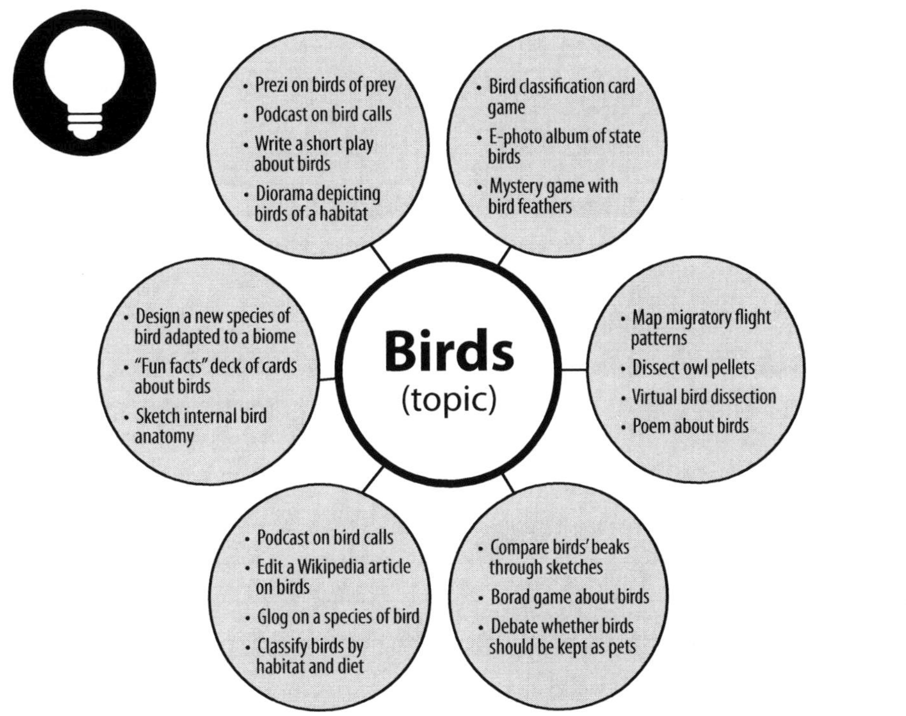

Figure 13. Creative idea generator in science.

who find texting under their desks more engaging than listening to their teachers and professors or memorizing factual material for a forthcoming test.

Another development in technology that aids infusion is the unlimited amount of information now available through the Internet. Thousands of free course-related materials are easily accessible through organizations such as the Khan Academy, which has produced more than 4,000 videos on topics across all grade levels and several curricular areas. The Massive Open Online Courses sponsored by some of the best-known universities in the country, including MIT's OpenCourseWare program and those available at Coursera, have produced thousands of courses that can be widely accessed without cost.

Changing the learning process has become a reality due to the unlimited access to the knowledge sources mentioned above. Teachers, however, can also become creative contributors to the resource stockpile and the producers of their own televised lectures, course-related material, and media events. Free or inexpensive software now enables teachers to prepare and upload their own lectures and assignments for student use anytime and anywhere through the application of easy-to-use screen casting software (e.g., Camtasia Studio 8, Screenflow Software).

A program called Juno (http://gofrontrow.com/en/juno) enables easy recording of high-quality audio/video clips without adding any extra work to a teacher's day. The program automatically adds titles and prepares files for uploading that can then be accessed by computers, tablets, smartphones, or interactive white boards. In addition, as mentioned above, content recorded by others is readily available in all subject areas. These resources enable teachers to easily turn their lectures and related lesson planning tools into audio and video podcasts and printed course and video materials that can then be uploaded for student access. We can capitalize on students' fascination and skills with technology and the availability of vast amounts of online material by giving teachers the license and ability to infuse creativity and thinking skills activities into standards-driven curriculum.

Although it is not practical to use infusion for every topic or course, this approach makes learning more engaging and creates an enthusiasm for learning that seldom results from covering curricular material in traditional ways. The guidelines for infusion are easy to follow:

- Select an activity that does not always have a single, predetermined correct answer.
- Find things that students do rather than sit and listen to.
- Give students choices that they will enjoy pursuing.
- Select activities that have various levels of challenge to which interested students can escalate.

Finding activities for infusion is now easier than ever. Internet-based search engines allow teachers to enter topics, subtopics, and sub-subtopics by subject area, grade level, and difficulty level. Thousands of high-engagement activities that enable teachers to locate and infuse an almost endless array of exciting enrichment activities can be found with this new technology.

Preparing for the Infusion Process

In the example related to the topic of birds above, the teacher used infusion activities in order to engage students' enthusiasm for learning in science. A traditional brainstorming technique and the Creative Idea Generator presented in Figure 13 were infused into the lesson in order to engage students and to come up with as many ideas as possible for making the teaching of this topic more interesting. Guidelines for brainstorming were briefly discussed (see Appendix

C) and teachers were asked to apply as many of the following criteria as possible to the brainstorming process:

1. The activity has a relationship to one or more regular curriculum topics.
2. There is not a single, predetermined correct answer or solution to the problem raised in the activity.
3. The activity consists of something students do, rather than sit and listen to.
4. The activity is fun for most students.
5. The activity should lead to some form of product development on the parts of students.
6. The activity has various levels of challenge to which interested students can escalate if they would like to creatively extend the interest through follow-up activity.

Students were then given an opportunity to select an activity that they would like to pursue based on their individual interests and learning styles. Most students chose to work in groups, however, a few students preferred to work on their own. Infusion activities can not only make a traditional, memory-oriented topic more interesting, but they can also present opportunities for developing creative, analytic, and investigative learning skills. Students learn cooperative, collaborative, and other executive function skills, strategies for acquiring J-I-T information, and most importantly, that learning is, in and of itself, an enjoyable process.

A Note on Problem-Based Learning

Problem-based learning (PBL) has gained a good deal of attention for making the curriculum for students more engaging. We are strong supporters of this approach to enhancing learning material in the regular (prescribed) curriculum. We do not, however, view it as creating the same experience as is the case with Type III Enrichment in the triad model. Generally speaking, and we know there are many variations on the use of PBL, teachers can use it to cover a standard curricular topic (e.g., natural selection in biology). There are expected outcomes that will probably show up on an end-of-unit test and perhaps even on a standardized achievement test. If the PBL approach makes the work more interesting and engaging, then such an approach has merit.

Type III Enrichment, however, is different because of the four requirements that make the problem more relevant to student interests, learning styles, expression styles, and the investigative methods that students choose to select and pursue a topic of their own interest and methodology. These are the factors that contribute to the personalization of learning and advanced-level investigations or creative endeavors. You'll recall that the four requirements of a *bona fide* Type III Enrichment project are as follows:

1. personalization of interest—the student(s) selects the topic,
2. use of authentic methodology—involves some kind of original data gathering or creative expression,
3. no existing solution or "right" answer, and
4. designed to have an impact on an audience other than or in addition to the teacher.

Summary

Someone once asked us what is the "value" of infusing these activities into the curriculum? We answered, "High engagement and involvement activities are remembered long after the facts, or dates, or formulas you learned in fourth period math or social studies are forgotten." An infusion-based approach to education and learning allows teachers to find resources within the school, community, classroom, and in the people who reside within the community that will enable them to *select* highly engaging enrichment-based activities related to particular topics, *inject* them into the curriculum to make the topics more interesting, and provide support and encouragement for individuals and small groups who would like to *extend* their pursuit of enrichment activities. The Schoolwide Enrichment Model provides a framework to enrich the learning opportunities for students within a classroom where state standards or the NGSS are present and must be addressed and incorporated into the lessons. By infusing prescribed standards with the richness of what lies beyond the standards or textbook, the academic and creative experiences of students become three-dimensional, as they recognize that the world is much bigger, and much more exciting than they could have ever imagined.

A quote by Nancie Atwell, the winner of the 2015 Global Teacher of the Year Award (considered by many to be the Nobel Prize for educators) is a good way to summarize the role that teachers can play in making science come alive in our classrooms. We end with her comment at the award ceremony about the importance of infusion.

> Teachers are people who can't imagine doing anything else; it's their passion. If there's nothing else you can ever imagine yourself doing, be a teacher. If you're passionate about making a difference in this world, be a teacher. A passionate teacher will find ways to infuse creativity and fun into learning, even amid the demands of testing and curriculum. But if the thought of teaching doesn't light you up—if you think it's just a job—don't go into education. There are more than enough teachers like that already. Am I trying to discourage my students from becoming educators? No. But I don't want to encourage someone to pursue a teaching career if the thought of working with children, teaching from the heart and the intellect, and making a difference in the lives of others doesn't light them up. No matter how bright a student is, no matter the GPA, we don't need people entering the field who aren't on fire. Because frankly, it's that fire that often lights our way when the horizon grows dark and ominous.

How do we teach from the heart and intellect and light the fire in our own mind that is mentioned in the above quote? When all is said and done, teachers who are knowledgeable about the ideas discussed in this book and who have the motivation and courage to infuse creative teaching in their own unique ways will inspire a love of science in their students and provide them with the opportunities that will produce many of the future's world-class scientists.

References

Adams, C., & Callahan, C. (1995). The reliability and validity of a performance task for evaluating science process skills. *Gifted Child Quarterly, 39*, 14–20.

Amabile, T. (1983). *The social psychology of creativity*. New York, NY: Springer-Verlag.

American Society for Engineering Education. (2014). *Science and engineering apprenticeship program*. Retrieved from http://seap.asee.org

Bandura, A. (1977). *Social learning theory*. Englewood Cliffs, NJ: Prentice Hall.

Barron, F. X., Montuori, A., & Barron, A. (Eds.). (1997). *Creators on creating: Awakening and cultivating the imaginative mind*. New York, NY: Putnam.

Bloom, B. S. (1954). The thought process of students in discussion. *Accent on teaching: Experiments in general education*, 23–46.

Bluestamp Engineering. (2015). *What is Bluestamp?* Retrieved from http://www.bluestampengineering.com/program-details

Bruner, J. S. (1960). *The process of education*. Cambridge, MA: Harvard University Press.

Bruner, J. S. (1966). *Toward a theory of instruction*. Cambridge, MA: Harvard University Press.

Burns, D. E. (1998). *SEM network directory*. Storrs: University of Connecticut, Neag Center for Gifted Education and Talent Development.

Chapin, S., O'Connor, C., & Anderson, N. (2003). *Classroom discussion: Using math talk to help students learn: Grades 1–6*. Sausalito, CA: Math Solutions.

Colangelo, N., Assouline, S. G., & Gross, M. U. M. (2004). *A nation deceived: How schools hold back America's students* (Vols. 1 & 2). Iowa City: The

University of Iowa, The Connie Belin & Jacqueline N. Blank International Center for Gifted Education and Talent Development.

College Board. (2015). *AP courses.* Retrieved from https://apstudent.collegeboard.org/apcourse

College Entrance Examination Board. (2003). *A brief history of the Advanced Placement program.* Retrieved from https://apstudent.collegeboard.org/apcourse

Compass Learning. (2013). *Renzulli learning.* Retrieved from http://renzullilearning.com

Dewey, J. (1913). *Interest and effort in education.* New York, NY: Houghton Mifflin.

Dewey, J. (1916). *Democracy and education.* New York, NY: Macmillan.

Donovan, M. S., Bransford, J. D., & Pelligrino, J. W. (Eds.). (1999). *How people learn.* Retrieved from http://ww.leadershipinnovationsteam.com/files/how_people_learn.pdf

Dotterer, A. M., & Lowe, K. (2011). Classroom context, school engagement, and academic achievement in early adolescence. *Journal of Youth and Adolescence, 40,* 1649–1660.

Feist, G. (2006). The development of scientific talent in Westinghouse finalists and members of the National Academy of Sciences. *Journal of Adult Development, 13*(1), 23–35.

Field, G. B. (2009). The effects of the use of Renzulli Learning on student achievement in reading comprehension, reading fluency, social studies, and science. *International Journal of Emerging Technologies in Learning (iJET), 4*(1), 23–28.

Flick, L., & Bell, R. (2000). Preparing tomorrow's science teachers to use technology: Guidelines for science educators. *Contemporary Issues in Technology and Teacher Education, 1*(1), 39–60.

Fowler, M. (1990). The diet cola test. *Science Scope, 13*(4), 32–34.

Gladwell, M. (2007). *Outliers: The story of success.* New York, NY: Little, Brown.

Godfrey, J. (2013). *New survey finds 85 percent of educational institutions allow BYOD despite security concerns.* Retrieved from http://www.bradfordnetworks.com/new-survey-finds-85-percent-of-educational-institutions-allow-byod-despite-security-concerns

Greenwood, C. R. (1991). Longitudinal analysis of time, engagement, and achievement in at-risk versus non-risk students. *Exceptional Children, 57,* 521–535.

Heilbronner, N. (2008). Science safaris: Developing bold academic explorers outside the science classroom. *Science Scope, 31*(7), 23–27.

Heilbronner, N. (2013a). Creating and delivering differentiated science content through wikis. *Science Scope,* 6(5), 24–34.

Heilbronner, N. (2013b). Raising future scientists. *Gifted Child Today,* 36(2), 114–123.

Heilbronner, N. H. (2014). Think instruments, think apps: Using app-based technology in the science classroom. *Science Scope,* 37(9), 2–9.

Institute for Broadening Participation. (2015). *Pathways to science.* Retrieved from http://www.pathwaystoscience.org/programs.aspx?u=HighSchool_High%20School%20Students&sa=either&p=either&c=either&submit=y&adv=adv&all=all

International Baccalaureate Organization. (2015). *About the IB.* Retrieved from http://www.ibo.org/en/about-the-ib

Kaplan, S. N. (2009). The grid: A model to construct differentiated curriculum for the gifted. *In* J. S. Renzulli, E. J. Gubbins, K. S. McMillen, R. D. Eckert, *&* C. A. Little *(Eds.), Systems and models for developing programs for the gifted and talented* (2nd ed., pp. 235–251) Waco, TX: Prufrock Press.

Kaufman, J. C., & Sternberg, R. J. (Eds.). (2006). *The international handbook of creativity*. Cambridge University Press.

Lancour, K. L. (2008). Science process skills for life. *Training Guide.* Retrieved from http://www.tufts.edu/as/wright_center/products/sci_olympiad/pslsl_training_hammond. pdf

Lehrer, R., & Schauble, L. (2006). Scientific thinking and scientific literacy. In W. Damon, R. Lerner, K. A. Renninger, & I. E. Siegel (Eds.), *Handbook of child psychology* (6th ed., Vol. 4). Hoboken, NJ: Wiley.

Leo, O., Quinn, H., & Valdes, G. (2013). *Science and language for English language learners in relation to Next Generation Science Standards and with implications for Common Core Standards for English language arts and mathematics.* Retrieved from http://www.nextgenscience.org/sites/ngss/files/Appendix%20F%20%20Science%20and%20Engineering%20Practices%20in%20the%20NGSS%20-%20FINAL%20060513.pdf

Machlup, F. (1980). *It's creation, distribution and economic significance, Vol. I.* Princeton, NJ: Princeton University Press.

Magnet Schools of America. (n.d.). *Awards.* Retrieved from http://www.magnet.edu/awards

Michaels, S., Shouse, A. W., & Schweingruber, H. A. (2008). *Ready, set, science! Putting research to work in K–8 classrooms.* Washington, DC: The National Academies Press.

Miller-Sadker, D., & Zittleman, K. R. (2013). *Teachers, schools, and society* (10th ed.). New York, NY: McGraw-Hill.

National Academies Press. (1996). *National science education standards.* Retrieved from http://www.nap.edu/read/4962/chapter/1

National Governors Association Center for Best Practices, & Council of Chief State School Officers. (2010). *National governors association and state education chiefs launch common academic standards.* Retrieved from http://www.nga.org/cms/home/news-room/news-releases/page_2010/col2-content/main-content-list/title_national-governors-association-and-state-educatio n-chiefs-launch-common-state-academic-standards.html

National Research Center on the Gifted and Talented. (n.d.). *How to develop an authentic enrichment cluster.* Retrieved from http://www.gifted.uconn.edu/sem/semart01.html

National Research Council. (2012). *A framework for K–12 science education: Practices, crosscutting concepts, and core ideas.* Committee on a Conceptual Framework for New K–12 Science Education Standards. Board on Science Education, Division of Behavioral and Social Sciences and Education. Washington, DC: The National Academies Press.

Next Generation Science Standards. (2013). *The Next Generation Science Standards.* Retrieved from http://www.nextgenscience.org/next-generation-science-standards

Neisser, U. (1979). The concept of intelligence. In R. J. Sternberg & D. K. Detterman (Eds.), *Human intelligence* (pp. 179–189). Norwood, NJ: Ablex.

NGSS Lead States. (2013). *Next generation science standards: For states, by states.* Washington, DC: The National Academies Press.

Olenchak, F. R. (1988). The Schoolwide Enrichment Model in the elementary schools: A study of implementation stages and effects on educational excellence. In J. S. Renzulli (Ed.), *Technical report on research studies relating to the revolving door identification model* (2nd ed., pp. 201–247). Storrs: University of Connecticut, Bureau of Educational Research.

Olenchak, F. R., & Renzulli, J. S. (1989). The effectiveness of the schoolwide enrichment model on selected aspects of elementary school change. *Gifted Child Quarterly, 32,* 44–57.

Padilla, M. (March, 1990). The science process skills. Research matters—To the science teacher. *National Association of Research in Science Teaching No. 9004.* Retrieved from http://www.narst.org/publications/research/skill.cfm

Perleth, C. H., Sierwald, W., & Heller, K. A. (1993). Selected results of the Munich longitudinal study of giftedness: The multidimensional/typological giftedness model. *Roeper Review, 15,* 149–155.

Piaget, J. (1975). *The development of thought: Equilibration on of cognitive structures.* New York, NY: Viking.

Reis, S. M. (2015). *Reflections on gifted education: Critical works by Joseph S. Renzulli and colleagues.* Waco, TX: Prufrock Press.

Reis, S. M., Burns, D. E., & Renzulli, J. S. (1992). *Curriculum compacting: The complete guide to modifying the regular curriculum for high ability students.* Waco, TX: Prufrock Press.

Reis, S. M., & Renzulli, J. S. (1982). A case for the broadened conception of giftedness. *Phi Delta Kappan, 64,* 619–620.

Reis, S. M., Westberg, K. L., Kulikowich, J., Caillard, F., Hébert, T. P., Plucker, J. A., . . . Smist, J. M. (1993). *Why not let high ability students start school in January? The curriculum compacting study* (RM93106). Storrs: University of Connecticut, The National Research Center on the Gifted and Talented.

Renzulli, J. S. (1976). The Enrichment Triad Model: A guide for developing defensible programs for the gifted and talented. *Gifted Child Quarterly, 20,* 303–326.

Renzulli, J. S. (1977). *The Enrichment Triad Model: A guide for developing defensible programs for the gifted and talented.* Mansfield Center, CT: Creative Learning Press.

Renzulli, J. S. (1978). What makes giftedness? Re-examining a definition. *Phi Delta Kappan, 60,* 180–184, 261.

Renzulli, J. S. (1982). What makes a problem real: Stalking the illusive meaning of qualitative differences in gifted education. *Gifted Child Quarterly, 26,* 147–156.

Renzulli, J. S. (1986). The Three-Ring Conception of Giftedness: A developmental model for creative productivity. In R. J. Sternberg & J. E. Davidson (Eds.), *Conceptions of giftedness* (pp. 53–92). New York, NY: Cambridge University Press.

Renzulli, J. S. (1988). The multiple menu model for developing differentiated curriculum for the gifted and talented. *Gifted Child Quarterly, 32,* 298–309.

Renzulli, J. S. (1994). *Schools for talent development: A practical plan for total school improvement.* Mansfield Center, CT: Creative Learning Press.

Renzulli, J. S. (2002). Emerging conceptions of giftedness: Building a bridge to the new century. *Exceptionality, 10*(2), 67–75. http://www.tandfonline.com/doi/pdf/10.1207/S15327035EX1002_2

Renzulli, J. S. (2005). The Three-Ring Conception of Giftedness. In R. J. Sternberg & J. E. Davidson (Eds.), *Conceptions of giftedness* (2nd ed., pp. 246–79). New York, NY: Cambridge University Press.

Renzulli, J. S., Gentry, M., & Reis, S. M. (2014). *Enrichment clusters: A practical plan for real-world, student-driven learning* (2nd ed.). Waco, TX: Prufrock Press.

Renzulli, J. S., Heilbronner, N. N., & Siegle, D. (2010). *Think data: Getting kids involved in hands-on investigations with data-gathering instruments.* Waco, TX: Prufrock Press.

Renzulli, J. S., & Reis, S. M. (1985). *The Schoolwide Enrichment Model: A comprehensive plan for educational excellence.* Mansfield Center, CT: Creative Learning Press.

Renzulli, J. S., & Reis, S. M. (1994). Research related to the Schoolwide Enrichment Model. *Gifted Child Quarterly, 38,* 2–14.

Renzulli, J. S., & Reis, S. M. (1997). *The Schoolwide Enrichment Model: A how-to guide for educational excellence* (2nd ed.). Mansfield Center, CT: Creative Learning Press.

Renzulli, J. S., & Reis, S. M. (2014). *The Schoolwide Enrichment Model: A how-to guide for educational excellence* (3rd ed.). Waco, TX: Prufrock Press.

Renzulli, J., & Reis, S. (2007). A technology based program that matches enrichment resources with student strengths. *International Journal of Emerging Technologies in Learning (iJET), 2*(3), 1–12.

Renzulli, J. S., & Smith, L. H. (1978). *The compactor.* Mansfield Center, CT: Creative Learning Press.

Renzulli, J. S., Smith, L. H., & Reis, S. M. (1982). Curriculum compacting: An essential strategy for working with gifted students. *The Elementary School Journal, 82,* 185–194.

Renzulli, J. S., Smith, L. H., White, A. J., Callahan, C. M., Hartman, R. K., & Westberg, K. L., . . . Systma-Reed, R. (2013). *Scales for rating the behavioral characteristics of superior students* (Rev. ed.). Waco, TX: Prufrock Press.

Reyes, M. R., Brackett, M. A., Rivers, S. E., White, M., & Salovey, P. (2012). Classroom emotional climate, student engagement, and academic achievement. *Journal of Educational Psychology, 104,* 700–712.

SciMathMN. (2015). *Instructional technology in science.* Retrieved from http://scimathmn.org/stemtc/resources/science-best-practices/instructional-technology-science

Sosniak, L. (1985). Becoming an outstanding research neurologist: Phases of learning. In B. Bloom (Ed.), *Developing talent in young people* (pp. 348–408). New York, NY: Ballantine Books.

Sternberg, R. J. (1984). Toward a triarchic theory of human intelligence. *Behavioral and Brain Sciences, 7,* 269–287.

Sternberg, R. J. (1988). Three facet model of creativity. In R. J. Sternberg (Ed.), *The nature of creativity* (pp. 125–147). Boston, MA: Cambridge University Press.

Sternberg, R. J. (1990). Thinking styles: Keys to understanding student performance. *Phi Delta Kappan, 71,* 366–371.

Sternberg, R. J. (2007). A systems model of leadership: WICS. *American Psychologist, 62*(1), 34–42. doi:10.1037/0003-066X.62.1.34

Sternberg, R. J., & Davidson, J. E. (Eds.). (1986). *Conceptions of giftedness.* New York, NY: Cambridge University Press.

Sternberg, R. J., & Davidson, J. E. (Eds.). (2005). *Conceptions of giftedness* (2nd ed.). New York, NY: Cambridge University Press.

Sternberg, R. J., Kaufman, J. C., & Pretz, J. E. (2002). *The creativity conundrum.* New York, NY: Psychology Press.

Subotnik, R., & Steiner, C. (1993). Adult manifestations of adolescent talent in science. *Roeper Review, 15,* 164–169.

Sydell, L. (2010). *Sci-fi inspires engineers to build our future.* Retrieved from http://www.npr.org/templates/story/story.php?storyId=129333703

Thorndike, E. L. (1921). Intelligence and its measurement. *Journal of Educational Psychology, 12,* 124–127.

The Virtual High School. (2014). *The virtual high school.* Retrieved from http://www.thevhs.org

Wang, M.-T., & Holcombe, R. (2010). Adolescents' perceptions of classroom environment, school engagement, and academic achievement. *American Educational Research Journal, 47,* 633–662. doi:10.3102/0002831209361209

APPENDIX A

Table Cross-Referencing Standards With Activities

NGSS Standard or Practice	Activity	Page
NGSS Standard MS-PS4-2—Develop a model to describe that waves are reflected, absorbed, or transmitted through various materials.	Maria must study sound waves to understand how to develop a solution to the problem of soundproofing a pet crate.	8
NGSS Crosscutting Practice 1—Defining Problems	Maria develops a problem that requires a solution—a soundproof pet crate.	8
NGSS Crosscutting Practice 2—Developing Models	Maria develops a model to test her solution to the soundproof pet crate.	8
NGSS Crosscutting Practice 3—Planning Investigations	Maria develops a plan for how to test her model.	9
NGSS Crosscutting Practice 4—Analyzing and Interpreting Data	Maria collects data on her model.	9
NGSS Crosscutting Practice 5—Using Mathematics and Computational Thinking	Maria tests her model mathematically.	9
NGSS Crosscutting Practice 6—Designing Solutions	Maria designs and tests a solution.	9
NGSS Crosscutting Practice 7—Engaging in Argument From Evidence	Maria uses data collected during her observations to support that her soundproof idea was a success.	9
NGSS Crosscutting Practice 8—Obtaining, Evaluating and Communicating Evidence	Maria evaluates her dog crate and decides how to market it.	9

NGSS Standard or Practice	Activity	Page
NGSS Standard 4-LS-1-1 Construct an argument that plants and animal have internal and external structures that function to support survival. NGSS Crosscutting Practice 1—Defining Problems NGSS Crosscutting Practice 3—Planning Investigations	Dan must investigate the sun's impact on skin and patterns of diseases associated with sun exposure to better understand the problem.	98
NGSS Crosscutting Practice 4—Analyzing and Interpreting Data NGSS Crosscutting Practice 5—Using Mathematics and Computational Thinking	Dan organizes and analyzes online data to discover a pattern that he will address in his solution.	98
NGSS Crosscutting Practice 6—Designing Solutions	Dan develops a solution to the problem—a product that will appeal to children and make them want to wear sunscreen.	98
NGSS Crosscutting Practice 7—Engaging in Argument From Evidence	Dan and Dr. M. test the solution and discover it seems to be having the effect that they had hoped—more children are wearing sunscreen.	98
NGSS Crosscutting Practice 8—Obtaining, Evaluating and Communicating Evidence	Together, Dan and Dr. M. evaluate the evidence, make improvements, and market the product.	98
NGSS Standard HS-LS3-2 Make and defend a claim based on evidence that inheritable genetic variations may result from: (1) new genetic combinations through meiosis, (2) viable errors occurring during replication, and/or (3) mutations caused by environmental factors.	Carla must study genetics and genetic variations to understand how genes impact whether or not an individual will develop a certain muscular disease.	99
NGSS Crosscutting Practice 1—Defining Problems NGSS Crosscutting Practice 3—Planning Investigations	Carla identified a problem—no one had used technology to analyze the genetic patterns for this muscular disease. She plans her investigation around this problem.	99
NGSS Crosscutting Practice 2—Developing Models	She must develop a predictive model and determines how well the data fit the model.	99

NGSS Standard or Practice	Activity	Page
NGSS Crosscutting Practice 4—Analyzing and Interpreting Data NGSS Crosscutting Practice 5—Using Mathematics and Computational Thinking	Carla uses mathematics and technology to test her model.	99
NGSS Crosscutting Practice 7—Engaging in Argument From Evidence	Carla uses the results of her data analysis to argue that the model is sound.	99
NGSS Crosscutting Practice 8—Obtaining, Evaluating and Communicating Evidence	Carla communicates her results through the Siemens Competition.	99
NGSS Standard MS—ESS3-3 Apply scientific principles to design a method for monitoring and minimizing a human impact on the environment.	Carolina investigates the impact of boating (human impact) on manatees (natural environment).	103
NGSS Crosscutting Practice 1—Defining Problems	Carolina notices some manatees' backs are scarred by boats.	103
NGSS Crosscutting Practice 3—Planning Investigations	Carolina must observe boaters to define the nature of the problem—when and why it's occurring. She conducts observations to understand the problem.	103
NGSS Crosscutting Practice 4—Analyzing and Interpreting Data	Carolina notices a pattern in the data that supports a hypothesis about why the collisions are occurring.	103
NGSS Crosscutting Practice 6—Designing Solutions	Carolina and her teacher develop ideas for solutions.	111
NGSS Crosscutting Practice 1—Defining Problems	Hikers notice that there are no plant guides for the hike that they are on.	103
NGSS Crosscutting Practice 6—Designing Solutions	Hikers design a solution—a smartphone app for a trail guide that hikers could download and use on the trail.	104

APPENDIX B

Internships, Apprenticeships, and Mentorships for Students in Science

Organization	Name of Program	Student Level	Program Description	Website
American Society for Engineering Education	Science and Engineering Apprentice Program	High school	Provides research internships to high school seniors to participate in summer research at Naval laboratories.	http://seap.asee.org
Appalachian State University	Future Engineers Camp	K–12	Provides students with a fun and positive introduction into various fields of engineering by using hands-on, creative investigations and real-world building activities.	http://nccet.appstate.edu/future-engineers-camps-2015
Arizona State University	COMPUGirls	8–12	Participants learn how to manipulate the latest technologies in digital media, game development, and virtual worlds to positively affect their communities.	http://universitydesign.asu.edu/db/compugirls-awakening-girls2019-passion-for-social-justice-and-technology
Arthritis Foundation	Summer Science Internship Program	High School	Through this internship, students receive hands on experience in the fields of rheumatology and immunology, with a focus on arthritis and related autoimmune diseases. Interns participate in either basic laboratory (bench) research or clinical translational/epidemiological (patient outcomes oriented) research.	http://www.kintera.org/htmlcontent.asp?cid=619297
Auburn University	Academic Enrichment Camps	K–12	The university offers more than 100 summer programs designed to educate and inspire youth in a variety of academic, athletic, and extracurricular endeavors.	http://www.auburn.edu/outreach/opce/auburnyouthprograms/academiccamps.htm
Baylor University	Summer Science Research Program	College freshmen	The program gives incoming freshman hands-on research experience by working on research projects with Baylor University science professors in many disciplines	http://www.baylor.edu/summerscience
Biotech Partners	Biotech Academy	High school	Students receive a comprehensive bioscience-based education and job-training skills. By completing the program, students earn a Certificate of Achievement in Bioscience.	http://www.biotechpartners.org/students.html
BlueStamp Engineering	BlueStamp Engineering Summer Research	High school	Hands-on engineering program operating in New York City, Houston, and San Francisco designed by industry professionals to show high school students the world of engineering first hand.	http://www.bluestampengineering.com

Organization	Name of Program	Student Level	Program Description	Website
Boston Leadership Institute	Three-Week Research Programs	K–12	Three-week STEM research programs are offered in a variety of areas, including STEM entrepreneurship, applied physics, biomedical fields, biological research, engineering, marine biology, chemistry, clinical psychology and psychiatry, and neuroscience.	http://www.bostonleadershipinstitute.com/research-programs.html
Boston University	CityLab's SummerLab Biotechnology Program	High school	Provides students with a hands-on experience and the freedom to design and plan their own experiments, while providing the support to help them learn from their mistakes.	http://www.bumc.bu.edu/citylab/summerlab
Carnegie Mellon University	Alice Workshop for Girls	6–9	Alice Workshop for Girls is a 2-week class that introduces middle school girls to computer science through an easy-to-learn program that allows them to create their own stories and games in 3D computer animation.	http://programming4girls.com/about_the_workshop.html
Carnegie Mellon University	National High School Game Academy	High school	Local video industry professionals help students discover new ways that video game techniques are being used.	http://admission.enrollment.cmu.edu/pages/pre-college
Carnegie Science Center	Summer Camp	K–12	During a week of themed activities and hands-on exhibits, students investigate science careers, experiment with roller coasters, build a bridge, and more.	http://www.carnegiesciencecenter.org/programs/summer-camps
Clemson University	South Carolina Commissioner's School for Agriculture	High school	Each college-based program provides an academically focused curriculum that integrates subject matter from a variety of related disciplines with the overall theme of agriculture and natural resources.	http://www.clemson.edu/cafls/sccsa
Coastal Studies for Girls	Semester School and Summer Programs	10	CSG is dedicated to girls who have a love for learning and discovery, an adventurous spirit, and a desire to challenge themselves.	http://www.coastalstudiesforgirls.org
College of the Atlantic	Summer Field Institute for High School Students	11–12	Students explore the connections between science, art, and the humanities while they engage in an intensive program combining academic work with field experiences.	http://www.coa.edu/highschoolstudentprograms.htm
Cornell University	CURIE Academy	High school	The CURIE Academy is a one-week summer residential program for high school girls who excel in math and science and want to learn more about careers in engineering. Cornell University's faculty and graduate students lead participants in classes, lab sessions, and project research.	http://www.engineering.cornell.edu/diversity/summer/high_school/curie/index.cfm
Cornell University	CATALYST Academy	High school	The CATALYST Academy is a one-week summer residential program for rising high school sophomores, juniors, and seniors. The mission of the CATALYST Academy is to advance diversity in engineering and its related disciplines.	http://www.engineering.cornell.edu/diversity/summer/high_school/catalyst/index.cfm

Organization	Name of Program	Student Level	Program Description	Website
Drexel University	Drexel University Computing Academy (DUCA)	High school	DUCA is a 5-week, residential, summer computing program at Drexel University in Philadelphia, PA, that promotes interest in information technology, computer science, business, and digital arts and media.	http://www.ducomputingacademy.org/index.aspx
Field Museum, University of Chicago	Stones and Bones: A Practicum in Paleontology	High school	Students will be introduced to important concepts in geology, paleontological method, stratigraphy, and Earth history. They will learn about basic techniques for the study of evolutionary biology including comparative skeletal anatomy of fishes and other freshwater animals, and examine methodological concepts such as fossil preparation, illustration, and description.	https://summer.uchicago.edu/high-school/stones-and-bones
Florida Institute of Technology	Marine and Environmental Science Summer Camp	K–12	This camp includes a 5-day odyssey of discovery exploring Brevard County's coastal ocean, the Indian River Lagoon, and local area creeks.	http://camps.fit.edu/dmes/index.php
Florida State University	Young Scholars Program (YSP)	Rising senior	YSP is a 6-week residential science and mathematics summer program for Florida high school students with significant potential for careers in the fields of science, technology, engineering, and mathematics, who have completed the 11th grade and are entering their senior year.	http://www.bio.fsu.edu/ysp
Georgia Tech	ECE Outreach	High School	This one-week summer program is designed to introduce students to electrical and computer engineering (ECE) concepts. The goal of the program is to instill an interest in ECE and increase the number of high school graduates majoring in this field.	http://www.ece.gatech.edu/academics/outreach/hot-days/index.html
Great Lakes Science Center	Family Programs and School Break Camps	K–12	Get your hands messy with family science experiments, analyze fingerprints to solve a "crime," build a robot using the latest LEGO NXT technology, explore the night sky, earn a Scout badge or spend the night among your favorite exhibits.	http://www.greatscience.com/programs.aspx
Howard University	CAREERS Weather Camps	High School	CAREERS consist of a network of summer science camps with a primary focus on atmospheric/weather and climate sciences for high school students.	http://ncas.howard.edu/outreach-programs/weather-camp
Hurricane Island Foundation	Summer Science and School-Year Programs	High School	Hurricane Island offers science and leadership programs in the STEM disciplines, marine ecology, botany, ornithology, island and environmental studies, ocean monitoring and research, and sustainable design and technology.	http://www.hurricaneisland.net/2016-programs

Organization	Name of Program	Student Level	Program Description	Website
Iowa State University	George Washington Carver Summer Research Internship	High School	The internship program promotes "science with practice" by exposing interns to research opportunities under the direction of faculty members. Disciplines commonly providing opportunities include agricultural engineering and studies; agronomy; animal science; various biology fields; entomology; food science and human nutrition; genetics; horticulture; natural resource ecology and management; plant pathology and microbiology; and sociology.	http://www.diversity.cals.iastate.edu/gwc
Jackson Laboratory	Summer Student Program	High School	This program provides high school students with an opportunity to conduct independent research under the guidance of staff scientists. More than 2,000 students, including three Nobel Laureates, have participated in the program.	http://education.jax.org/summerstudent/index.html
Leadership Education and Development	LEAD Summer Engineering Institute (SEI)	High School	The SEI immerses students early in their academic development and exposes them to innumerable career opportunities in engineering and computer science. The program equips them with knowledge and expertise from our nation's leading universities and corporations, empowering students to confidently make better informed decisions when choosing their university and career.	http://www.leadprogram.org
Lehman College	Women in Science Program	High school	Select students participate in a 6-week program, where they take one course in either biology, chemistry, environmental science, or computer science.	http://www.lehman.edu/new-science-building/women.php
Maine Medical Center	Summer Student Research Program	High School	During the 10-week summer internship period, students participate in mentored research projects either in basic science laboratories or working with physicians at Maine Medical Center to impact patient care or treatment outcomes.	http://mmcri.org/summerstudent
Maine School of Science and Mathematics	Summer Camp	Ages 10–14	Through hands-on interactive classes and thrilling extra activities, campers will be challenged to explore their favorite subjects, learning that there's more to math and science than meets the eye!	http://www.mssm.org/page.cfm?p=541
Massachusetts Institute of Technology	Research Science Institute (RSI)	High School	RSI is a cost-free, summer science and engineering program that combines on-campus course work in scientific theory with off-campus work in science and technology research.	http://www.cee.org/research-science-institute

Organization	Name of Program	Student Level	Program Description	Website
NASA Pennsylvania Space Consortuim	Grade 9–12 Student Opportunities	High School	The programs offered here include a Junior Academy of Science competition, academic and career exploration, a precollege engineering course, exploration days, summer camps, and other opportunities.	http://pa.spacegrant.org/9-12-student-opporrtunities
National Institutes of Health	Diversity in Vision Research and Ophthalmology (DIVRO)	High School	The DIVRO program offers each participant the opportunity to work closely with leading research scientists in the Division of Intramural Research and provides students with hands-on training in a research environment that will prepare them to continue their studies and advance their careers in basic and clinical research.	https://www.nei.nih.gov/training/diversity_in_research
National Science Foundation	Summer Research Apprentice Program (SRAP)	High School	SRAP is an intensive, 6-week, paid summer research program held at the University of Wyoming.	http://www.uwyo.edu/epscor/fellowships-and-student-programs/srap/index.html
Northeastern University	The Young Scholars Program	High School	The Young Scholars Program offers future scientists and engineers a unique opportunity for hands-on experience while still in high school. The program is open to Boston-area applicants who have completed either their sophomore or junior year in high school.	http://www.youngscholars.neu.edu
Ocean Exploration Trust	Honors Research Program (HRP)	High School	HRP students work with scientists and engineers to learn about oceanography, data visualization techniques, and the scientific research process. After completing a research project on shore based on data collected by Nautilus, HRP students participate in seagoing expeditions to work with the Corps of Exploration and stand watch as Data Loggers alongside scientists and engineers.	http://www.oceanexplorationtrust.org/#!honors-research-program/ca78
Pacific Northwest National Laboratory	Student Research Apprenticeship Program (SRAP)	High School	The SRAP is a research-based educational internship experience for students who are members of ethnic groups traditionally underrepresented in science and engineering (Hispanic, African American, or Native American).	http://science-ed.pnnl.gov/default.aspx?topic=Student_Research_Apprenticeship_Program
Rochester Institute of Technology	Co-Internships and Summer Research Opportunities	High School	This is a listing of mostly paid internships and other research opportunities for students across the country.	http://people.rit.edu/gtfsbi/Symp/highschool.htm
Rockefeller University	Summer Science Research Program (SSRP)	High School	High school students gain hands-on research experience in Rockefeller University laboratories over their summer break. Each SSRP participant is mentored by a Rockefeller scientist who works side-by-side with the student to run experiments, develop, gather, and analyze data, and formulate results.	http://www.rockefeller.edu/outreach/summer_science

Organization	Name of Program	Student Level	Program Description	Website
Roswell Park Cancer Institute	Summer Research Internship Programs in Cancer Science	High School	Each student spends 7 weeks working full-time on an independent research project under the supervision of a of RPCI scientific staff member and alongside graduate students and postdoctoral trainees.	https://www.roswellpark.edu/education/summer-programs
Rutgers University	Toxicology, Health & Environmental Disease (THED) High School Summer Program	High School	THED is an intensive, week-long, nonresidential program in which students will participate in a variety of laboratory activities such as DNA isolation, PCR, cell culture, gel electrophoresis, enzyme activity measurement, and microscope slide staining, in addition to discussions about careers in medicine, pharmacy, toxicology, environmental science, and research.	http://eohsi.rutgers.edu/content/toxicology_health_environmental_disease_high_school_summer_program_0
Sandia National Laboratories	Internships & Co-ops	High School	Interns work on real-world, challenging projects; they also socialize, travel, and explore life in New Mexico and California.	http://www.sandia.gov/careers/students_postdocs/internships
Santa Fe Institute	Summer Complexity and Modeling Program (CAMP)	High School	Through individual projects, computer simulation activities, analysis of ecological data, lectures and seminars, along with related weekend activities, students conduct research in this cutting-edge field. Days are made up of instruction, small working group sessions, and research time interleaved with sports and extracurricular events.	http://santafe.edu/education/schools/summer-camp
Shoals Marine Laboratory	Summer courses	High school	Laboratory exercises and field work will include explorations along Appledore Island's rocky intertidal zone and excursions to neighboring islands to observe harbor seal and seabird colonies.	http://www.sml.cornell.edu/sml_students_highschool.html
Smith College	Field Studies for Sustainable Futures	High School	This is a 2-week residential program for the environmentally conscious student. Participants learn about sustainable living, environmental science and environmental policy in a hands-on, interactive, project-based program. Much of the program is conducted in the field, and includes hiking, camping, visiting local farms, and touring new buildings that conform to the highest environmental standards.	http://www.smith.edu/summer/programs_sustainability.php
Smith College	Summer Science and Engineering Program	High School	This is a 4-week residential program for exceptional young women with strong interests in science, engineering, and medicine. Each July, select high school students from across the country and abroad come to Smith College to do hands-on research with Smith faculty in the life and physical sciences and in engineering.	http://www.smith.edu/summer/programs_ssep.php
Sonoma State University	Summer High School Internship Program	High School	Select students spend 4-6 weeks working with instructors at Sonoma State University. They participate in research projects in a variety of fields and receive stipends for their work.	http://www.sonoma.edu/scitech/hs

Organization	Name of Program	Student Level	Program Description	Website
South Dakota State University	ACE Camp	High School	At the camp, students will receive at least one hour of flight training, get behind the controls of an aircraft, launch a space shuttle using a computer generated flight simulator program, build and launch air rockets, map orbits of planets, graph sun spots, visit with pilots, and ride in a hot air balloon.	http://www.sdstate.edu/cs/undergraduate-programs/aviation/aerospace-career.cfm
Stanford University	Stanford Medical Youth Science Program (SMYSP) Summer Residential Program	High School	Hospital internships, anatomy laboratories, and lectures provided by Stanford faculty expose students to hands-on science and a variety of health, medicine, and science careers.	http://smysp.stanford.edu/education/summerProgram
Sweet Briar College	Explore Engineering for High School Women	High school	These events are a great way to see what engineering is all about. During each camp, students stay with college mentors.	http://sbc.edu/engineering/explore-engineering-high-school-women
Synthetic Biology Engineering Research Center	Introductory College Level Experience in Microbiology	High School	The program seeks to broaden students' in understanding of biotechnology and the careers available in this field. In addition to basic science and research, the program also exposes students to career exploration and preparation for the college application process, including field trips to local biotech companies, career talks with scientists and engineers, writing a college personal statement, meeting college admission and financial aid experts, and visiting college campuses. Open to students near Berkeley, CA, only.	http://synberc.org/iclem
Texas A&M University	WE IDEAS Summer Camp	High School	This residential summer program is designed to give female high school students with an interest in science, mathematics, and engineering an opportunity to explore engineering as a career.	http://engineering.tamu.edu/easa/camps/we-ideas-summer-camp
TRUE Dive Team	Teen Research Underwater Explorers (TRUE)	High School	These hands-on experiences with marine ecology and SCUBA diving are designed to promote science, active stewardship and conservation of our oceans and coasts, while also building citizenship and leadership capabilities for future generations.	http://www.truediveteam.org
University of Arizona	KEYS High School Summer Internship Program	High School	The 7-week KEYS program is a unique summer opportunity for motivated high school students with a strong interest in bioscience, engineering, environmental health, or biostatistics. After a week of training in laboratory techniques and safety, interns participate in research projects under the guidance of University of Arizona faculty and other laboratory members.	http://keys.pharmacy.arizona.edu/index.php

Organization	Name of Program	Student Level	Program Description	Website
University of California, Los Angeles	CNSI Nanoscience Lab Summer Institute	High School	During this 5-day program, students have the unique opportunity to explore questions similar to those currently investigated by the scientific community. The program involves hands-on experiments that combine vigorous scientific methodologies and techniques with projects that are both fun and exciting.	http://www.summer.ucla.edu/institutes/NanoScienceLab
University of Chicago	Research in the Biological Sciences	High School	This 4-week intensive training program is designed to expose students to a broad range of molecular, microbiological, and cellular biological techniques currently used in research laboratories. Students will be immersed in the research experience, giving them a taste of life at the bench. Using a project-based approach, the course progresses from a survey of basic lab techniques to the application of current molecular techniques in developmental biology and microbiology.	https://summer.uchicago.edu/high-school/ribs
University of New Hampshire	High School Summer Internship Program	High School	This 7-week program presents an overview of computer technology and offering hands-on experiences in a real-world networking facility. Summer interns are exposed to the computer science, electrical engineering, and computer engineering disciplines programs offered by the University of New Hampshire.	https://www.iol.unh.edu/students/highschool-internship
Waynflete School	Sustainable Ocean Studies	High School	A 24-day summer program focused on promoting ocean sustainability, Sustainable Ocean Studies blends hands-on learning with adventure as participants do important work on pressing issues related to ocean sustainability.	http://waynflete.org/sos

APPENDIX C

Guidelines for Brainstorming

1. Introduce the question to be brainstormed and review the rules of brainstorming:
    a. All ideas are welcome.
    b. No comments, criticism, or evaluation during the brainstorm.
    c. The more ideas, the better.
    d. Don't worry about duplicate ideas at this point.
    e. Piggybacking on each other's ideas is encouraged.

2. Explain what will be done with the brainstormed ideas. Write the question to be brainstormed at the top of the first page of flipchart paper or on the board.
3. If you wish, offer a one-minute "quiet period" before the brainstorm for people to think about the question and jot down a few ideas.
4. Begin the brainstorming.
    a. Guide the brainstorm by recording ideas on a flipchart or whiteboard as they come. You may wish to designate a recorder. Stop any comments that evaluate ideas. Invite new ideas, and encourage the group to share their ideas freely. Help generate energy and free-thinking through encouragement.
    b. As the responses slow down, offer last chances for additional ideas, then stop the brainstorm. Ask the recorder for his or her ideas. Thank people for participating.

5. Ask for clarification of any ideas that are not clear to you or others.
6. Discuss ways that the ideas can be presented to students in appealing ways (e.g., dramatizations, role-playing, artistic or pictorial representations, debates, games, friendly competitions, storytelling, digital graphics, 3D printing, film making, Facebook or Twitter exchanges, community service projects, entrepreneurial endeavors, etc.).

About the Authors

Nancy N. Heilbronner, Ph.D., is the Interim Dean at the School of Education at Mercy College, New York. Dr. Heilbronner's research is in the field of gifted and science education, and her work includes *Think Data, Think Instruments, Let's Be Scientists,* and *Ten Things Not to Say to Your Gifted Child, One Family's Perspective,* which was honored with the Parent's Choice and Texas Legacy Book Awards.

Joseph S. Renzulli, Ed.D., is a distinguished professor of educational psychology at the University of Connecticut and director of the Neag Center for Creativity, Gifted Education and Talent Development. The American Psychological Association named him among the 25 most influential psychologists in the world and in 2009, Dr. Renzulli received the Harold W. McGraw, Jr. Award for Innovation in Education.